BUZZ

BUZZ

HOW TO GROW YOUR SMALL BUSINESS USING GRASSROOTS MARKETING

GEORGE AFFLECK

*To my partner in life and at work, Amanda Bates, and to
my kids, Evelyn, Piers, and Quinn. But also to my dad, Allan Affleck,
who taught me more than he ever knew.*

Curve Communications
www.curvecommunications.com

Cover design by Kevan D'Agostino
Interior design by Peter Cocking and Nayeli Jimenez

Cataloguing data is available from Library and Archives Canada

Contents

· · · · · · · ·

Section 4: Taking Stock of Your Marketing Budgets and Plans

How This Book Works

. . . .

THIS BOOK IS structured to concisely and easily describe the different ways a business can market itself. It's written to be a step-by-step guideline for your marketing campaigns. Reference the appropriate sections and subsections, and follow those steps to carry out your campaign. Whether you need to write a press release, prepare for an interview, plan a media buy campaign, or set up a pay-per-click campaign, you'll be able to reference this book for step-by-step instructions. The book is divided into two broad subjects: online advertising and traditional advertising and publicity. It then ends with some resources to help you flesh out your marketing strategy, such as a marketing plan template.

Buzz will teach you how to run marketing campaigns, including pitching stories to the media, writing press releases, creating posters, setting up Facebook ads, or increasing your site's SEO. I don't expect you to use every strategy I lay out for you. By reading the descriptions and step-by-step outlines, you'll have a strong understanding of how to set up and run your own marketing campaign.

Introduction

The $2 Latte—Marketing Techniques That Will Really Grow Your Business

．．．．．．．．

WOULD YOU BE interested in a $2 latte? Would that offer—possibly heard on the radio or at the watercooler—tempt you away from Starbucks and into a new coffee shop? Of course it would.

That simple idea—and the marketing behind it—transformed a coffee shop from a single struggling location into a highly successful local franchise with ten cafes and millions of dollars in sales.

Through my agency's proven Buzz Formula, I'll show you how your small business can have that kind of success with even the most minimal budget (the marketing budget for the coffee shop was $10,000, including my agency fee).

Buzz will show you how to

- analyze your business's marketing budget for maximum results;
- use the tools of the marketing trade to get customers through the door; and
- make more money with less.

My Buzz Formula isn't rocket science or a get-rich-quick formula—it's composed of proven techniques that will help you grow your business.

Over the past fifteen years, my agency has worked with hundreds of small businesses, non-profits, and event organizers. We've helped businesses and organizations get people to walk through the door, RSVP for their events, or pick up the phone and call. The budgets for these clients were all over the map, but the one thing they had in common is the Buzz Formula worked for all of them.

Start Local

ONE OF THE themes of this book is to start local and build from there. We'll provide you with a Buzz Formula for local success that you can then extrapolate to markets across your region, your country, and even your continent. That coffee shop is now a chain with ten cafes around town, but they got liftoff by concentrating on people who worked within a block of their first shop.

Whether you're a coffee shop with a great latte in a mid-sized town or the organizer of a boat show in a major market, the techniques I provide will have people banging down your door for your product or service.

But Let's Get Back to That $2 Latte

THE $2 LATTE is an example of how a local business with a good brand can take a little marketing budget and ride it into the stratosphere.

About five years ago, a family who had decided to expand their business approached my agency. They owned a successful high-end restaurant in the city, but saw a future in coffee. My first reaction was to ask them if they were serious and why they had chosen the most competitive industry in North America, dominated by the all-powerful Starbucks. But they were clear about their goals, and, as a marketer, I believe that if a business owner has a clear goal and a great product, we're already 90 percent of the way there.

Simply put, they said their coffee was better than the competition's, and they were designing a space that would be more welcoming than a Starbucks.

Well, they were right about the coffee—it *was* great. And the space *was* very cool.

Right away, the biggest challenge was getting people to change their habits. How could we make them turn left instead of right when they got off the morning train to the office? *Come to us, not Starbucks!* Changing habits is a marketer's worst nightmare.

With a tight budget—$10,000 total, including my agency fee—I knew this would be tough. So, as we always do, my team sat down and brainstormed. We had to find one single thing that would resonate on the street, in ads, at the watercooler at people's offices, and when pitching to media.

We knew the coffee was great—we just had to get people to try it *once*. And their lattes—the shop's best and most expensive drink—was their crown jewel. So we focused on that, but, at $4, the price point was high. Most people only ordered lattes if they were splurging. The rest of the time, they ordered a regular coffee, which, at this shop, was still great—just not *latte* great.

Then we came up with it. If we could make the latte so cheap that people would stop and go, "Wow, I gotta get one of those," then we knew we were on our way.

Once the owners agreed to sell lattes for $2 for the foreseeable future, we got to work on the marketing plan. Curve has always believed that a multifaceted marketing campaign will produce the best results. That's why we approach our clients' needs by thinking about all the options: the best public relations (PR) outlets, web design, social media presence, and media buys. We love new media, but we also appreciate the value of old-fashioned methods like billboard advertising and local newspapers. We've worked with enough small businesses over our fifteen-plus years to know they value efficient campaigns that get the most for their dollar.

We decided to use our Buzz Formula with the coffee shop. This formula works best when budgets are tight and you need to concentrate your advertising so that the consumer thinks you're bigger than you are. It's a way to kick-start marketing in the hope that more sales will then lead to a healthier marketing budget in the future, if needed.

With retail launches like this, we use our Buzz Formula's 30/30/30/10 rule. This works really well at the planning stage.

The basic philosophy is that before you start spending money on ads online or offline, before you start planning an event, before you start thinking about the PR potential, you should divide your budget into 30 percent for radio, 30 percent for TV and/or outdoor ads, 30 percent for print and/or online, and 10 percent for a contingency. We've used this formula over and over, and it works every time.

Since we only had $10,000 for the marketing campaign, including our fee, thus leaving around $8,000, we had to be efficient.

The first thing we always start with is the creative. Advertising is part psychology, part art, and part promotion. It can be so subtle it's almost subliminal, or so blunt it comes off as insulting. Good advertising is both creative and amorphous—it doesn't talk down to the customer, but connects with them on a direct, gut level.

This one was easy—$2 lattes go straight to the guts (and wallets) of office workers. So we made sure the home page of the coffee shop's website was dominated by a story on the latte promotion. Then we created a very attractive print advertisement and an A-frame sign to sit out on the sidewalk—that ate up $1,500 of our budget.

Then we approached the major local daily newspaper— the one most people read on public transit—which offered us a print and online campaign for $3,000. These days print media are offering amazing services, including taking care of your Google AdWords, as well as your online and offline advertisements.

Next, we approached a local radio station to partner with us on the launch. The store was just across the street, so we offered some gift cards for the sales staff to use with their best clients. This helped us triple the $2,500 we were placing at the radio station for the radio advertisement.

Then, we put about $1,000 in elevator TV advertising in several office towers within a block of the store (people won't go much farther than a block for their hit of caffeine).

Public relations is a powerful tool every business should use to increase their profile. Today's consumer is constantly tapped into the news. Newspapers, smartphones, e-readers, blogs, podcasts, and social media sites such as Twitter and Facebook magnify news stories through horizontal or "viral" communication. The consumer is now the medium, and small publicity pieces can yield huge results through social media.

So we had to figure out the PR spin. We lucked out. It turned out that one of the owners—the youngest kid in the family—was an award-winning latte art barista. That was PR gold. We were able to pitch him to local TV stations, where he did the latte art on location. He was amazing—hearts, faces, names—the guy could do crazy things with foam and coffee. We also pitched him to radio and TV to talk about coffee culture and the art of the latte.

By the end of the one-month campaign, we had run six quarter-page ads, forty radio spots, and ongoing elevator ads, and had placed permanent A-frame sign on the street. Our PR was everywhere. We had taken the $10,000 investment and turned it into closer to $40,000 worth of promotional and PR value. There were lineups out the door.

Marketing works through repetition, but the first step is always the hardest. Once consumers get to know and trust your brand, the next steps are always a little easier.

The launch—and the first $10,000—was just the first step in the coffee chain's ongoing marketing campaign. The shop slowly raised the price of the latte until it was back at $4 a year later. However, the process had already taken place; we had changed the habits of coffee lovers in the vicinity of this shop. The best part was knowing that the formula could be replicated in every new market the chain opened in.

Five years and nine new shops later, the $2 latte formula is still working for every opening. In fact, people now know about the concept without us even telling them. Whenever a new shop opens, word of mouth spreads the news through the neighborhood: *Get down there, the lattes are only $2!*

How to Market Your Business Like a Pro

FOR MANY SMALL businesses, the glut of new marketing strategies available is simply overwhelming. Websites, blogs, Facebook, Twitter, LinkedIn, press releases, events, media buys—there are so many moving parts to marketing that many people don't even know where to start.

Buzz will help you understand the strengths—and weaknesses—of the different types of marketing, and show you how to undertake your own marketing campaigns efficiently and easily. It's written for small businesses with limited funds. You won't find suggestions on how to run a million-dollar marketing campaign or make a sixty-second commercial for the Super Bowl. What you'll learn, however, are the X's and O's of putting together a successful marketing strategy regardless of your budget, business, or expertise. *Buzz* will help you grow your business, whether through SEO, social media, public relations, or advertising.

Most businesses don't have the budgets of huge brands, like Coke or McDonald's, but if you own a business you'll need a marketing budget. You may think your business is so great it'll survive on word of mouth alone. But, really, that's rare. Even if you're a business that may grow because people just want your product or service (restaurants are good example of this), you still need to market yourself to set you apart from the thousands of other restaurants just like yours.

As a business owner, you may be suffering from information overload. Are you tempted by the latest shiny objects—the ones that are sold as quick fixes that will guarantee to make you a millionaire?

Our Buzz Formula will help you cut through the noise and decide what to focus your time, energy, and (oh-so-limited) dollars on. We're here to bring you back to earth, because, the truth is, there are no quick fixes, and sometimes those shiny objects are just distracting you from marketing principles that will increase customers and sales.

The Buzz Formula works especially well for start-ups that just need that initial push. However, it also works well for ongoing businesses and franchises that have limited budgets, but need to keep reminding the customer that they're out there fighting for their dollars.

As we make our way out of this rough economic period, don't you want to be ready to crush the competition? Get ahead of the Curve and build your business for the future?

I can give you all the tools for success, using our unique Buzz Formula to maximize every marketing dollar you have.

Sell those properties.

Promote that event.

Be the $2 latte coffee shop that's now making millions.

SECTION I

The Buzz Formula and How to Generate Buzz for Your Business

OUR BUZZ FORMULA is a way to kick-start your marketing in the hope that more sales will lead to a healthier, ongoing marketing budget, if needed. It is best used when budgets are tight and you need to concentrate your advertising so that the consumer thinks you're bigger than you are.

But, before I describe the formula or tell the story of the real estate launch, I want to tell you my story: how I came to be a storyteller and then a marketer, and what I learned along the way.

· 1 ·

My Story

· · · · · · · ·

AS A BUSINESS owner or entrepreneur, you do work that is part of a larger journey. Most successful entrepreneurs I know are addicted to learning, because they know that if they stand still for too long, the business world will pass them by.

I got my first taste of being an entrepreneur when I was ten years old. My parents had just moved the family to a small town because they wanted to escape the busy side of the big city. So I found myself in an area far outside the city where my dad could still practice real estate and we four kids would have the space to grow up and—hopefully—stay out of trouble.

My dad was a huge inspiration for me. He truly believed that the free market society we lived in was the greatest, and, with the right energy and desire, amazing success was within anyone's grasp, if they really wanted it.

I would listen to my dad's life lessons about how business works. How companies make profits. How customers or clients can be found. How to close a deal.

I decided to launch my own business at the young age of ten. It felt like a logical thing to do because my parents were the kind of 1970s parents that let us have the freedom to explore and learn—and work hard—but they didn't give us an allowance. We were told that if we wanted money, we had to earn it. Because my mom and dad had shown me how to use the lawn mower, the barbecue, and several power tools, I knew I had some skills to sell and I knew there was a demand for at least one of them: lawn cutting.

So I knocked on all the neighbors' doors and offered to cut their lawns for $6. These were big lawns—half an acre each—and I was only about four foot four, but I was tenacious. After my first time knocking on doors along the country road, I had two customers secured for one-time trials.

Despite my diminutive size, I could power through a half acre in a couple of hours, and, because watering lawns wasn't banned in the summer back then, the grass had to be cut twice a week. My trial with those two lawns went well, and, before July hit, I was making $24 a week cutting two lawns.

Then my business *really* took off. While getting those first two customers took a lot of hard work and convincing (i.e., marketing and sales), word of mouth (i.e., PR) spread the news.

Pretty soon I had eight neighbors wanting me to cut their grass. I was smart enough to know I couldn't manage this on my own, so I asked a few friends if they would be willing to help (my first staff). I would pay them $4 a lawn and keep $2 for negotiating the deal. By mid-August, I had eight lawns being cut by my friends twice a week, and I was making $32 a week for doing nothing but manage the staff (my friends) and collect the money from my neighbors. Of course, I didn't get off scot-free—my parents still made me cut their lawn for no charge.

Still, the entrepreneurial bug had bit me, and, in 1974, $32 a week for a ten-year-old was darn good money. And I had learned about marketing, sales, management, accounting, and PR, all in one go. Needless to say, my dad was very impressed.

These basic lessons have stuck with me throughout my careers, and they still apply to my clients today. I love the fact that my business career started in the grass-cutting business, because I believe *grassroots marketing* is the most successful and measurable communications strategy a business can have.

My Wandering Years and What They Taught Me

THROUGHOUT MY TEENS, I always had plans to become a business owner, with a backup plan to go into politics. My parents raised us four kids to question authority (remember, it was the 1970s). We were taught to argue and debate, so Sunday dinners were always lively, with my mom starting debate topics with both pro and con sides.

After graduating from high school, I enrolled in business school at university. But, when I was in my third year in 1985, my dad passed away from a massive heart attack at forty-nine years old. His death sent me into a tailspin that had me questioning the point of working so hard if you could die so young.

I was twenty-one and lost. I dropped out of university, saved enough money from working to buy a plane ticket to Europe, and started a personal exploration that would last many years.

I travelled to the UK, Egypt, Israel, Turkey, and all over Europe. Then, after two years of wandering, I decided to come home and go back to school.

I contemplated picking up where I had left off, but realized that I had lost my passion for business. So I switched to English, thinking that reading books and debating with my fellow students would at least be more fun.

Inspiration from an Unlikely Source
(AKA Grandma to the Rescue)

SOMETIMES YOU DON'T realize you've had a life epiphany
until long after it's happened. Just after I returned home, my
grandmother became very ill. Nana, as we called her, was my
mom's mom, and my sisters and I were all close to her because
she had helped raise us. We often went to her for advice. She
was quite a character and a party favorite when I was growing up because she was a concert pianist and liked to read my
friends' futures using playing cards. And, believe me, I'm a skep-
tic when it comes to fortune-telling and other new age mumbo
jumbo, but she was accurate. Truly and spookily accurate.

Nana got sicker and sicker and soon reached the point of
no return. I was alone with her in her hospital room near the
end. She asked me very quietly what I was planning to do now
that I was back. My response was vague and non-committal.
And then I asked her if she could see what would happen to
me. Could she predict my future?

She took my hand in hers, squeezed, looked me in the eyes,
and said, "Now George, if I tell you what is to happen, you'll
miss the plot. The journey is the fun part." She paused before
adding, "All that really matters is that you do what you love.
Then you'll get to where you need to be."

Nana died later that day. That same month, I graduated with
a degree in English, which didn't qualify me for many jobs.
However, I was lucky enough to fall into journalism, and was
soon building a career as a producer in public radio.

While the work was interesting and diverse, working for
a large bureaucratic corporation took its toll. Things moved
slowly, and deep down I knew that I didn't really fit in. Creativity and new ideas weren't coveted; in fact, being different
or doing things your own way were often seen as threats.

I had to get out of there!

Leaving was like leaving the mafia. They kept pulling me back in for contracts that were hard to say no to. By this time I was married and had a one-year-old baby, so I had to extract myself slowly. The first step in doing this was to become a freelance writer and broadcaster. Most writers aren't good at sales, but it was in my blood. I immediately used the same techniques I had used for my lawn-cutting business all those years ago: market to your audience (in this case print media and broadcasters), have a good brand (I was known for writing funny pieces), and know how to advertise (pick up the phone and call).

My career flourished, and I had the best of both worlds. I was free and finally doing something I loved. The big problem was that the margins were terrible. I soon realized my income would be capped by what I could produce myself in the hours that a day had. I could increase the rate I was charging, but knew I would never make enough.

So I decided to go over to the dark side...

The line between journalism and PR is thin. So I knew I could make this work, using my contacts, the right business model, and my ability to sell.

I launched Curve Communications in 2000. I didn't want it to be a PR-only company. Because of the work I had been doing as a writer, I had learned and seen firsthand that the media landscape was changing. The Internet offered huge potential, and the line between advertising and PR was getting blurry.

So Curve Communications would be a full-service marketing and communications agency. While I knew little about some of the service areas, I was a quick study, and I also knew—just like when I was ten years old—that there were talented people in the market who could help me address my clients' needs.

· 2 ·

Use the Buzz Formula as a Starting Point for Your Grassroots Marketing Campaign

· · · · · · · ·

ONE-STOP MARKETING SHOPS were still unique back in 2000. A lot of businesses would hire a PR firm, a website designer, an advertising agency, and so on. I had been working as a journalist for so many years, had been pitched to by PR people—usually badly—so many times, that I knew I could do better. And, when I started looking at potential clients, I noticed many that would really benefit from the expertise of my new agency.

As a writer, the first thing I did before agreeing to do a story was to look at a company's website. If the site was weak and represented the company badly, I would always pass. I would also look at how the company presented itself through its advertising and design. So many times, these companies lacked cohesion. The company—or event, or service—might have been a leader in their field, but their messaging was often weakened or confused by poor web and print design, bizarre media buys, lousy writing, and other terrible practices. These companies' CEOs may have had a great story to tell, but when it came time to tell that story, they needed some serious help.

When I created Curve Communications, I knew that the agency's skill set—our competitive advantage—would be client storytelling. It was an instinctive approach, because that was exactly what I had been doing as a journalist. I also knew that if my company was able to tell the client's whole story—allow it to flow through all of the company's creative and marketing material—it would be so much more than just PR. If you know your story, brand, or product, getting customers to come through the door or pick up your product becomes so much easier. I came up with a formula for marketing success early on: my Buzz Formula. In recent years, the advent of social media has made my holistic approach to storytelling and marketing even more relevant, but it hasn't changed the basic principle. I realized if my clients focused on the customer base within a ten- to twenty-kilometer radius of their brick-and-mortar business, they would maximize their success, regardless of what business they were in. This formula can then be easily expanded from market to market and adapted to any budget, from $10,000 a year to more than $100,000.

This book will take you on a journey. It'll tell you the story of how my established grassroots marketing techniques have been helping small businesses succeed for over fifteen years, no matter their budgets. I'll take you through each of the marketing strategies that are crucial for business success. If you follow this formula, and all the components within it, you'll position your business as a leader in your community.

I'll introduce that Buzz Formula in a minute. But first I'll show you how we used it with a client of ours.

A few years ago, a real estate client asked us for help. Their situation was challenging. We implemented our Buzz Formula, which we also call the 30/30/30/10 rule, at the planning stage because it's always a great place to start building your campaign. We've used this formula over and over, and it works every time.

All service industries have been hit by the recent economic downturn, but real estate has seen particularly big ups and downs. That's why marketing has become so crucial to sales success. It's as simple as asking: what makes my development more appealing than any other?

In every corner of this continent, people are craving a more neighborly approach to homes. Sprawl is out. Or, if there's sprawl, it must include a community that people can feel connected to. The idea of Main Street is back in a big way, and real estate marketing has picked up on that theme big time.

Just take a look through your local newspaper. The ads for big developments seldom show the buildings—instead,they include lifestyle shots of people at a street café, kids in a park, or dinner parties with your friends and beautiful kitchen. Those images make you want to be a part of that carefree crowd. You say to yourself, "Yeah, that's me, walking down that sidewalk, laughing. Or with the kid in a stroller. Or drinking a martini. I *want* that!"

We know, at Curve, that lifestyle is the story that informs the brand. So when our agency was approached to help market the sales of apartments in a new development, we started—as usual—by asking the client to describe their brand.

They talked about the grocery store that had already moved in, the nearby parks and playgrounds, a pub, two restaurants, easy access to transit. They never mentioned what the apartments looked like, and, frankly, it didn't really matter. They had painted a picture of what life would be like in the community. They defined their brand by how people would experience the new development. Our marketing campaign needed to emphasize the lifestyle on offer.

The problem was that their budget was tight. While they had spent significant money on the construction, they were strapped for cash because sales just weren't happening. They had already done some advertising, but they still weren't feeling the buzz. They wanted a fresh approach, but they only had $30,000. That may seem like a big budget, but, with eighty units up for grabs, the profit margins were huge.

Since this was only phase one of the development's construction, most of the retail shops were empty. The potential for a vibrant neighborhood was there but not easy to see since it was not completed. We needed to give people an idea of what this neighborhood would be like in the future and not what it looked like at that time.

We determined that our core consumers or audience were young professionals and families with one or two kids who were okay with living in a high-density community. The challenge: how could we maximize our budget and make people believe there would be life in this little village-to-be?

The answer, we decided, was to hold a good old-fashioned street party. We needed free stuff and staff assistance, so we started with our retail partners that were already there and invested in the village's success. We set aside $10,000 for the event itself. It would be a one-day family event with free food, bouncy castles, face painting, lots of gift cards, and, of course, VIP tours of the homes.

Now that we knew what the event would look like, we had to make sure some people showed up. The benefit of holding an event to market something is it gives you a focus for your advertising and your PR. It has a beginning, a middle, and an end, which makes it much easier to budget for.

First we had to build a website. The company had a corporate website, but it lacked a clear focus on the community it was trying to sell. We didn't need a full website, just a basic, mobile-friendly microsite:
- a home page talking about the project, with a banner at the top listing the event details;

- a second page on the units for sale; and
- a "Contact Us" page.

That's it. We built that using a freelancer for $300.

With $20,000 left to market the event, we knew we would have to print various items, so we set aside $3,000—a rough guess, but our experience said it was plenty. That left us with $17,000.

The 30/30/30/10 Rule

WITH FULL-ON EVENTS like this, we use our Buzz Formula 30/30/30/10 rule. As we mentioned earlier, this works best at the planning stage. Before you pick up the phone to buy advertising, divide your budget into 30 percent for each medium, and leave 10 percent for a contingency. In this case, because we wanted to drive people to an event, we placed 30 percent in radio, 30 percent in TV and/or outdoor ads, and 30 percent in print and and some of their online products, and used our 10 percent contigency to top up online.

We knew who our target market was, and our instincts told us which media would be the best bet for reaching them. So we approached two stations with the $5,000 we had set aside for radio and asked them both to be our partners. We told them about the event and got two fantastic proposals back.

In the end, we went with the station whose audience matched our demographic best—and that had the higher ratings. They promised us they would broadcast live from the event all day, run several ads on the station in the two weeks leading up to the event, and provide bonuses that included ads on their websites, email blasts to subscribers, and mentions on the morning show all week. We paid them $5,000, but the total value of everything they gave us was closer to $15,000, so we tripled our investment. We were very pleased with this.

Next, we approached the best TV station in town with $5,000, no more and no less (salespeople actually *love it* when you're clear like that). TV advertising is expensive, but for $5,000 we could get several ads sponsoring weather (you've seen them—"weather brought to you by Main Street Bank. Get your mortgage today"). We also were added to their weekly listings, where they put four or five listings together and created a TV ad saying something like, "this week in your town, check out these fun events."

We couldn't convince them to guarantee a live story from the site—$5,000 doesn't go *that* far—but they did throw in a free interview on their morning show so the development company's CEO could talk about this exciting new neighborhood and plug the event too. Basically, free PR. The total value of what they gave us exceeded $10,000, so we doubled our investment.

Then we went to the local daily and weekly papers. Newspapers really can't always add a ton of value promotionally, so it comes to down to rate—how much each ad is going to cost. We negotiated hard and got the price down by 50 percent, doubling our investment again.

We knew we needed some outdoor exposure, but we couldn't afford transit or billboard ads. So we printed three hundred posters with details of the event and hired some students (found on Craigslist) to post them all over town one week before the event, and again the day of.

We also printed some postcards and had them put in coffee shops, libraries, and other places within a three-mile radius. We even placed these postcards in the mailboxes of current owners in the neighborhood because we wanted them to join us and meet their future neighbors.

We had 10 percent left—around $2,000—so we put that into Google and Facebook ads. These two online media are fantastic for reaching a specific demographic when there's a clear call to action. In this case, the event was the focus, but we also wanted to get people talking about this new community—really get the buzz going out there.

The event was a success and the weather behaved (although we had rented tents, just in case). The free food, bouncy castles, prizes, and advertising convinced 900 people to show up that day, and most of them toured the apartments for sale. Two weeks later, the client had closed numerous deals worth several million dollars. That gave them the leeway to afford an ongoing advertising campaign. The entire village is now a flourishing, coveted place to live. The little one-off community event is now held every summer and has become a regional attraction.

Small Businesses Can Do Their Own Marketing

AT CURVE COMMUNICATIONS, we believe marketing should be built on a multi-disciplinary strategy. Those who have the greatest success do so by developing relationships with their consumers through different marketing strategies. This can become quite overwhelming, which is why many people decide to pay others to do their marketing for them.

Large businesses often require an agency to handle marketing strategies, especially if the campaigns are on a national level. However, smaller businesses that are hoping to capitalize on a regional market are fully able to set up and run their own marketing campaigns. This not only saves them money, it also gives them direct control of their public image and puts them in daily contact with their customers—an invaluable resource in this age of social media and fast-moving trends.

You can do your own marketing—and this book will help you get started.

Why the Buzz Formula Is a Great Place to Start

I'VE SPENT A lot of time talking about these examples—both the coffee shop and the real estate development—because they focus on a core service that a lot of our techniques stem from. The coffee shop in particular, which was detailed in this book's introduction, is one example of how far you can stretch your marketing budget for your small business. You don't have to have millions to make millions. A strategic plan, and perhaps utilizing the Buzz Formula, can start you toward great success.

Over the years, our agency has marketed a ton of businesses and, specifically, events: boat shows, car shows, operas, ballets, cultural festivals, small expos, and so on. We've had big budgets and small ones, but our techniques were established and honed from years of experience. Marketing events provided us with the building blocks for grassroots marketing techniques that have also worked on non-event clients. In short, if your budget is limited, try thinking about the year as a succession of events. Whether it's once a year or several times, consolidating your funds for the most local exposure can work effectively for small- and medium-sized businesses. Think of how a major department store implements its marketing strategy when holding a sale—it is often referred to as a sales event. What they do is inundate the market promoting the event so the consumer cannot miss it—flyers, radio ads, TV ads, and on it goes. Your small business can create similar campaigns at a fraction of the cost.

The formula I described in the real estate case study tells it all. First determine your marketing budget—whether it's

$10,000 or $100,000 per year—and apply our Buzz Formula, which must include an event or gimmick, a time period, and, possibly, the use of the 30/30/30/10 equation—like the $2 latte. The formula works best when you have a limited marketing budget. It's all about maximizing the spend by being creative with your advertising, your media partners, and your PR, in order to promote an event, stunt, or gimmick.

Think of your event or launch as a way to concentrate your budget and maximize the results. It can be as simple as a $2 latte, or as big as a street party. It really depends.

So how will you decide to spend your limited marketing budget? When money is tight, you can't afford an agency like mine. You need to find a way to do it yourself, and knowing where to start can be daunting.

So let me tell you how the Buzz Formula works.

13 Steps to a Buzz Formula

1. **Decide exactly what you're marketing** (i.e., your brand and the thing that makes your business unique in the marketplace).
2. **Set your budget.** How much can you really afford? Being an entrepreneur is stressful, but you don't need to break the bank. Marketers use mathematical equations. Start-ups need to set aside 10 to 15 percent of their gross budget, and 5 to 7 percent once they're up and running. But, let's face it, business—especially small business—is driven by cash flow. That said, I would suggest that $10,000 a year is the minimum for marketing a brick-and-mortar business. Whether you spend every penny on SEO and Google ads or use our Buzz Formula, you'll need at least $10,000.
3. **Know your media terminology.** Do you know what advertising, media promotion, media buying, and media relations are?

There's some terminology that comes in handy in marketing, but a lot of it's just gobbledygook. For the Buzz Formula you only need to know a few things:

- Media buying is the most important part of advertising. It means spending money purchasing advertising space in newspapers, radio, TV, outdoor, online, and so on.
- Advertising design is what people usually mean when they say "advertising." It's the design part—what your ad will look or sound like. You need to work this out early on, because a nice chunk of your budget will need to go to it.
- Media promotion is added value from the media you're buying. Media outlets don't always have it, but you need to ask about it. They often have a person dedicated to coming up with cool promotions, because they need to market themselves too. They need partners, like you, to reach out to the community and stay relevant.
- Media relations—often called PR or public relations—is talking to the media about getting our story told. Talking to reporters is an art unto itself. But nothing beats free advertising, and getting an endorsement from a newspaper, TV, or radio reporter is a great way to establish yourself as a trustworthy business. In the mind of the consumer, if the media says it, it must be true.

4. **Identify two key people:** the face of the brand and the person who'll be in charge of the marketing file. This is crucial to stay organized, but, also, to have someone that'll be your go-to person, if the media wants to do a story on you.

5. **Get organized.** Use Excel to track everything. If you don't know how to use spreadsheets, learn. Now. In business, they're crucial.

6. **Research media in your town** (i.e., radio, print, TV, outdoor, and other). You know your product or service, so you probably have a good idea of what your customer is watching, listening to, or reading. Write down at least one of each type of media outlet,

and start thinking about outdoor advertising. Find the best places outside to advertise in your neighborhood: trains, billboards, posterboards, lightpoles, and so on.

7. **Decide if online is the right place for your business.** And, if so, where and how much of your marketing budget should it devour? Which channels do you want to focus on, and which ones do you want to ignore?

8. **Investigate creative and other marketing collateral** (i.e., rack cards, brochures, website, Facebook, etc.). At a bare minimum, you need some kind of online presence. It doesn't have to be a lot of material. Remember, in the real estate story I talked about a microsite: three pages, that's it.

9. **Divide up your media buy and determine when it should run.** This is the toughest part. Start with the 30/30/30/10 rule. Remember, this is a starting point. It puts things in perspective, especially when you find out how expensive one media outlet might be over another.

10. **Negotiate with traditional media.** Quite often they have posted or advertised rates for their ads, but the real prices are much lower. It's a lot like buying a car—you need to negotiate. Remember, it's *your* money and they're salespeople. Don't be intimidated just because they're the big TV or radio station in town. They need your money.

11. **Do your online media buying.** This is sometimes the most difficult part, and is often worth outsourcing. Thankfully, both Google and Facebook offer a lot of tools and services, including sales representatives, to help you out. And traditional media outlets, such as newspapers, sometimes offer to manage your online as well.

12. **Create a PR story.** This is a mystery to many of our clients. They don't know they have a story, but it's sitting right in front of them. Ask your friends what they find interesting about your business: is it the new concept, design, menu item, exotic

material? With the Buzz Formula, the gimmick or event being marketed is sometimes the story itself. You saw how we did this with the $2 latte.

13. **Track your success.** This part is tough. It's your business, and you know your goals. So, are more people coming through the door since you ran your campaign? If you're a service business, tracking online results is much easier nowadays, which will be covered in the chapter on Google AdWords and Facebook ads.

Who Is the Buzz Formula For?

OUR FORMULA WORKS best with businesses that already have a reputable brand and a solid base but are looking to grow and expand. It helps if you already know your business well and are willing to work to make it succeed even more.

The Buzz Formula is especially suitable for

- brick-and-mortar businesses that sell products or services;
- those that run small events, or who are coaches, authors, or consultants; and
- local business owners (e.g., retailers, dentists, financial service providers).

Our best clients already have a marketing and advertising budget, and they understand that they need to invest in themselves and their business to make more money, grow their business, and get to that next level.

Quite often, our clients create a success ratio. So, if they spend $10,000, they want to see their investment multiply. We've worked with restaurants that have required a ten times return, so, for $10,000, they want $100,000 back in new business. That's very ambitious. I would suggest you start with 2 to 1, or even 1 to 1 at the beginning, until you establish your brand and start building some buzz.

The Buzz Formula is *not* for
- people who are looking to get rich quick;
- people who like to complain and make excuses; and
- anyone who isn't serious about growing their business.

Take Advantage of a Stale Economy

MARKETING BUDGETS ARE often the first thing companies cut when facing financial troubles. Don't make that mistake. McGraw-Hill researchers followed 200 companies during the 1930 and 1980 recessions; they found *the companies that marketed the most had the biggest sales increases.* The same study showed the companies that spent the most during the recession grew 256 percent faster than their competitors—the ones who had cut their marketing budgets.

A 2001 study by Yankelovich/Harris showed marketing in a down economy made management and staff feel much more positive about a company's commitment to its products. Most importantly, those firms were top-of-mind when customers made purchasing decisions. If your competitor is a bigger company, they're likely to have taken a bigger financial hit during the downturn. Take this chance to catapult over them and stand out from the crowd while the economy is down.

Companies need to think of down periods as opportunities, not threats. Recessions are times when there isn't a lot of noise out there. Timing is crucial! Take advantage of a slower economy to grow your business and your brand!

Creating new, strong relationships with consumers takes time and dedication. Now is the best time to invest in your marketing, while the economy is slowly growing. Building your marketing strategies now will ensure that your business grows in time to take advantage of a strengthened consumer market!

So, let's get started and take your business to new heights.

9 Key Thoughts on Marketing

THIS LIST WILL help you think more like a marketer.

1. **Marketing today is built on an integrated approach.** Make sure your business has created the right marketing mix. PR, advertising, design, social media, and Google AdWords are all tools in your marketing toolkit.

2. **Don't believe the naysayers—you** *can* measure success! Google Analytics and Google searches allow you to see the momentum your marketing campaign is making, even if it hasn't shown up in your income statement yet.

3. **Online media is providing some of the most inexpensive advertising opportunities ever.** What's more, *you* can control the story being told about your company. This may not last long, so take advantage of it while you can. The online market is built for small businesses, and it'll allow for you to target specific demographics and psychographics better than ever before.

4. **Don't put marketing last on your list of priorities.** Marketing is the only way customers will know about your product or service. Studies show companies that invest the most in marketing succeed the most, while those that cut their marketing costs fail the fastest.

5. **Marketing is the surest way to build your business for the future.** Building a business is difficult. Building it to last is even more difficult.

6. **Always mine the resources, tools, and connections you've already created when beginning a new marketing campaign.** Existing Facebook and Twitter accounts, friends, acquaintances, and clients are all valuable resources for marketing your business.

7. **Research and development is the same for every aspect of your business—including marketing.** Don't feel bad about copying marketing programs that have worked in similar markets or

on similar products. Measure their success and tweak your own campaigns accordingly.

8. **Stay tuned to market changes.** For example, a recession opens and closes opportunities depending on what you're selling and how you sell it.

9. **Remember—marketing is more about conversation than promotion!** Listen to your customers, your service providers, and anyone else—they can tell you a lot about how you're doing, and how you should move forward. And now with social media, the conversation is more immediate, more extensive, and sometimes more impersonal, but social media acts like an ongoing market research tool that you can access for free easily. All in all, remember to work with your customers to build your business and increase sales.

SECTION 2

Optimizing Your Online Presence

ONE OF THE first hurdles we often face with potential clients is their apparent lack of concern for their online presence. They may have the greatest product or service in the world, but their website is pure garbage, their tweets are offensive, and their Facebook page is too personal.

Imagine, thirty years ago, if you were to pull out a crumpled up, coffee-stained business card and give it to a customer. What if you were to hand a customer a company brochure that was full of typos, terribly written text, and graphics that appeared to be hand drawn by your five-year-old? Weird? Ugly? Lazy? Yes. Now, imagine—thanks to the power of the Internet—you multiply that single experience by thousands, or millions. If it's not good business sense one-on-one, scaling it upwards is just ridiculous.

One of our recent clients in the financial services sector created a great product. It did everything right: it had great PR potential, it was event focused, and it catered to a hungry demographic that would gobble it up. It was a winner. I admit, we were so dazzled by the product that we neglected to look at their website in a holistic way. We realized this right away when we started pitching reporters to do stories on this revolutionary concept.

The first thing the reporters did, even while we were talking to them on the phone, was Google the company to see their online presence. All the stories and comments about the product were positive, but their website had let them down in a big way. As soon as the reporters saw the site, they would say, "Nah, looks too salesy. Maybe you should just buy an ad."

What they meant was the site was trying to "hard" sell. It had the price of the product in a massive font. The whole website looked like a cheap, late-night TV infomercial. Again and again, the site undermined our efforts every time we tried to talk to the media. It was truly frustrating, because we knew the product was great, but we just couldn't get past the editorial gates to get the kind of media coverage we were looking for. The client was disappointed and refused to change the site. As a result, we were disappointed because we couldn't achieve our own goals that were within such close reach .

This example shows just one of the ways your online presence can let your business down. Your website, social media, videos, photography, SEO, apps, and online advertising are your calling cards, not just for customers, but for media, other business partners, bankers, and even your competition. You have to get it right the first time—before any other steps are taken.

Building a Great Website

• • • • • • • •

NOT HAVING A great website is like wearing gray to a party filled with vibrant colors—you kind of just blend in or, worse, stand out for not standing out. Boring. Not having a website at all is like not being invited to the party—no one even knows you exist.

DO: Use eye-catching visuals.

DON'T: Use distracting GIFS or graphics.

DO: Include easy-to-find navigational links.

DON'T: Get cutesy with your link headers. There's nothing wrong with calling your e-commerce page "Store." Calling it "Where the Magic Happens" is confusing.

DO: Make sure your page loads fast.

DON'T: Overburden your site so it runs slower. On average, if a site doesn't load within three seconds, people click elsewhere.

DO: Make your page mobile-friendly, or offer a mobile version.

Your website is a digital business card. It should be filled with pertinent information, like who you are, what you do, and how to contact you. In fact, generally the "who we are" sections of websites are the most visited, so make yours good!

The desktop computer isn't going anywhere, but many of us now search for information on our phones. It's best practice to invest in a mobile-friendly site, especially if you offer sales via your website. In fact, as of April 2015, Google demands that your site be mobile optimized. If it's not, they say it'll affect your ranking in their search engine.

Your mobile site should just be a simpler version of your website. Keep the most important information available, like your phone number, store hours, and checkout page (for those who provide e-commerce).

Make your mobile site "one column." Remember you're targeting those who are navigating with thumbs! Make navigational links large and easy to click on. If you have a lot of navigational links on your desktop website, cut them back to the ones that a mobile user would need.

The impact of mobile, and how people experience a website, is still being analyzed. You can test your site for mobile readiness at google.ca/webmasters/tools/mobile-friendly.

Blogging

BLOGGING SHOULD BE an integral part of your website, because it shows your viewers (and Google) that you're an active website that's constantly updated with new, relevant information.

As a whole, blogging has come a long way from teenagers pouring out their daily thoughts into online journals. Blogs— and the bloggers who write them—have become sources for legitimate news. Regular blogging for your brand sets you up as an industry leader and can help set you apart from your competition. In fact, many corporate websites now use blogging to increase their influence.

The massive growth of WordPress, a simple programming language created initially for bloggers but now used by Fortune 500 companies, is a testament to the impact of blogging and your online presence.

Where to Start?

IT'S AN INCREDIBLY popular trend lately for companies to start up their own blogs and create their own content. The vast majority of these blogs target other companies and professionals who use the information to enrich their own knowledge and write their own blog articles.

So what's the point? Far too many people write blogs, create content, and go through the motions. Just because all the experts in the industry are doing it, they feel like they should too.

You need to figure out exactly why you do *anything* related to your business. If you're thinking of starting a blog, you need to understand why a blog is necessary and what you and your company hope to achieve from it.

Ideally, your content should be one step in a much larger process—or funnel—that will change users from viewers to customers. Being an established authority in your field, whatever your niche may be, comes with many benefits. The more that people in your industry perceive you as an expert, the stronger your brand will become.

Blogs don't need to be as complicated as *War and Peace*, and, in fact, they generally shouldn't. Our attention spans are getting shorter and shorter, so content needs to be both concise and engaging from the get-go.

1. **Have a blog page set up on your website.** A blog on your website can work well if you want people to stay on your site or you want them to get to know the personality of your organization.

Don't send people away from your site to other people's content; keep them there with your own captivating storytelling. Content management systems (CMS), like WordPress, are easy to install and use for even novice bloggers.

2. **Find the content.** Finding content for your blog posts is usually the hardest step. Keep your eyes open, though, because content is all around us—the key is finding a way to tie it in to *your* brand. You might even consider outsourcing the writing to a seasoned writer who's familiar with your industry.

3. **Write the content.** If you write the blog posts yourself and find yourself struggling with writer's block, there are a number of ways to get around it. Try writing anything that comes into your head. Take five minutes to jot down some thoughts. You'll find that little pieces start to form a full picture and can trigger a bigger, better idea. If all else fails, step away from your writing, grab a coffee, take a walk, and don't fret. Like many things, this is much easier said than done.

   - **Find your passion.** Choose a topic that you really care about, and write about it, even if it doesn't seem directly related to your industry. Can it be tied to your industry? Can it be tied to something happening in current events that could be related to your industry? If the topic is too much of a stretch to use in your blog, save the idea for later, and try to think of a different topic.
   - **Find your angle.** Find an angle that appeals to you. The topic "How to Use Facebook" is very generic and bland for a blog post. Be more creative, and try to find a more interesting story to tell. For example, "How These Companies Gained Thousands of Likes Without Spending a Cent in Advertising," or "Three Corporate Scandals that Destroyed These Companies' Brand Image."

     The more interesting the angle is for you, the easier it'll be to write. More often than not, my most popular articles have been ones that I've written without any prior planning. If you find yourself stuck on brainstorming a good topic, you can always look up similar blog titles from other companies in the industry. Don't plagiarize or copy anything, but see if you can find any inspiration from them.

- **Write first, edit later.** This is a particularly difficult practice for many writers. They keep writing and rewriting the first paragraph, but nothing seems good enough, and the article never really gets any traction. In my experience, sometimes it's better to just start writing, and worry about quality control afterwards. This can help unclog your mental processes and get the creativity flowing!
- **Leave it overnight.** Once you have your first draft written, leave it overnight. Editing with a fresh set of eyes in the morning will help you notice issues with sentence structure, grammar, and flow. If you're short on time, leave it for a couple of hours, at the very least, before getting back to it.

4. **Tag your blogs.** This allows your readers to find related content. Perhaps, you write frequently about bad weather. Tag relevant blogs with keywords like "snow," which, when clicked on, brings up all other blogs with that tag. This is a simple step that many corporate blogs sadly ignore.

3 Important Statistics About How People Are Responding to Blogs

1. Business blogging leads to 55 percent more website visitors. (Source: Hubspot.)
2. Social media and blogging account for 23 percent of all time spent online. (Source: Mindjumpers.)
3. B2B companies with blogs generate 67 percent more leads per month, on average, than non-blogging firms. (Source: Social Media B2B.)

Ultimately, how much you post is up to you, but it's best to keep your blogs consistent. Pick two or three days a week that you wish to publish your blog, and try to stick to this schedule. Don't be afraid to move your posting time around if the first time you choose doesn't appear to get much traction. Contrary to popular belief, there's no "magic time" to post anything. It greatly varies from business to business, and you need to find a time that works for you.

A Few Words About WordPress

CREATING A WEBSITE from scratch can be quite expensive. Furthermore, making changes to a custom-built website can be extremely cumbersome for those who don't have a professional background in web design. For small businesses, the best option may be to use a platform such as WordPress, which allows you to build your own website by plugging your content into ready-made templates.

WordPress is free and open-sourced, with a wide range of available themes, templates, and plug-in architecture. It's the largest blogging software on the web, powering 16.6 percent of all blogs and attracting more than 600 million visitors each month. WordPress is an excellent platform for making a quality website without spending too much money.

· 4 ·

SEO (Search Engine Optimization)

* * * * * * * *

WHEN YOU SEARCH for something on Google, such as "Vancouver best restaurants," which link will you click on? Will it be the first link that comes up? If the first one doesn't look good, you might scroll further down the page, but chances are you won't ever go to the second page.

If you're a business that wants to be noticed on Google—or whatever your search engine of choice might be—you need to be high up on the first page. That's where search engine optimization (SEO) comes in. To show you exactly how SEO works, I'll use imaginary clients to demonstrate how to create a straightforward strategy that can be applied to almost every business.

Imagine you own a shoe shop in Portland, Oregon. You need to make sure your website appears on the first page of results when a user searches "Shoe Shops Portland." How can you make that happen? If this sounds like some obscure, technical detail you probably don't need to bother with, don't be fooled. The answer lies in SEO, which is fast becoming the key to getting your business noticed online. You do need to bother with it. Here's why.

When somebody does search for the keywords "Shoe," "Shops," and "Portland," their search engine crawls through the entirety of the Internet, finding all the relevant websites and ranking them accordingly, based on their relevance to you. But while search engines like relevancy, they also like importance. This is where SEO comes into play! If you've built your shoe shop website properly, and it complies with the right search engine rules, Google will reward you by moving you higher in the search ranking and closer to the first page.

This chapter outlines the processes you can put in place to make sure your target audience finds you through search engines. Many of our recommendations will need to be executed by your web developer, so this chapter will also give you the information and language you'll need to speak with them. If you know and understand what needs to be done online, you'll be one step ahead of some of your competitors.

The "New" Yellow Pages

GONE ARE THE days when the local Yellow Pages phone book dominated the search for a business category. And, while Yellow Pages may not be down for the count, as they aggressively pursue online formats that may or may not work, I think we all know that online search, mostly via Google, is key to any business success.

This power shift has changed how consumers find local businesses, and why it's so important for your company to appear prominently in the results of local searches and listings sites that rank high on search engines. This isn't to say you should avoid Yellow Pages or other listing and review sites, like Foursquare, Angie's List, Yelp, and so on. Yellow Pages and other sites are starting to work with search engines to enhance their listings. If you're signed up on one of these directories, you'll be easier to find, and that's the key. If a customer can't find you, you're losing business from the start.

The 4 C's of Search Engine Optimization

SEARCH ENGINE OPTIMIZATION is a huge topic, so we'll just touch on the four C's of SEO before going into more detail further in the chapter.

Collection

ONE OF THE most important parts of SEO is making sure that every single page is consistent with its keyword. If you have a page with information on the benefits of tomato soup, make sure tomato soup is the central focus of the *entire* page.

The first step of any SEO effort is to find relevant keywords. Ideally, every page of your website should have a keyword. This is the central focus of your page, and it should be interspersed in the page title, the headers, the writing, and other page elements.

It's important to research which keywords are a good choice. Setting a keyword to "Blogging" will have you competing against a ton of other, different companies for the first page of Google's search rankings. Try to find a keyword that isn't too popular, but still conveys the message you want to send.

Content

LET'S BE HONEST, your site should have high quality content anyway! For maximum SEO, make sure your pages are long enough, well written, and easy to read. A good minimum length is 300 to 400 words per article.

Make sure to use plenty of images and videos (as long as they're relevant) in your posts to mix things up. In addition to the quality of the site itself, Google will track how long people stay on your page, so give people a reason to keep reading.

Clutter

KEEP THE CLUTTER to a minimum! While it's tempting to shoehorn your keyword into every single sentence, your writing will become awkward and stiff. Mention the keyword every now and then, but make it sound natural. Another big no-no is having excessive advertisements. Keep them tasteful and unobtrusive to avoid being penalized by Google.

Connect

ONE OF THE biggest determinants of SEO is having a lot of popular, reliable sites consistently linking back to you. Use your connections and contacts to spread your website across different networks for maximum effect. However, be very careful not to overly rely on shady guest bloggers. With the new changes to Google algorithms, businesses have to select their guest bloggers very carefully. Matt Cutts, the head of Google's Webspam team, says he wouldn't recommend accepting a guest blog post unless you're willing to vouch for someone personally or know them well. Likewise, I wouldn't recommend relying on guest posting, guest blogging sites, or guest blogging SEO as a link-building strategy. However, SEO isn't the be-all objective of your site. Not even the best SEO can salvage a poorly written website that no one wants to read.

Google It: How Internet Users Search Online

WHEN A USER searches online, they generally have a purpose. They may be looking for specific information or trying to find that cool bar they walked past. Your role is to make that journey as smooth as possible. Remember, the user is impatient, and she doesn't have any time to waste. If the information she wants isn't at her fingertips, she'll just go elsewhere.

Decide how users will be searching for you. Are they looking to buy a product from you or just looking for you to provide them with information? You can use this information to conduct keyword research (covered later on in this chapter), and use the keywords to create more effective copy. When a user lands on your website from their search query, you'll want them to say, "These are the guys I've been looking for."

One of the common mistakes advertisers and marketing teams make is misjudging the language their audience uses when searching online. You absolutely must use the same keywords as your target market.

Language misinterpretation can range from spelling variations (e.g., specialized versus specialised, color versus colour) to word association (e.g., cell phone versus mobile phone). Be sure to do a keyword analysis before you write your website copy.

The 3 Types of Search Queries

When you're writing website copy, keep in mind that users will approach your site in three different ways.

1. **Transactional queries:** this is a user actively seeking to buy a product or service (e.g., "Shoes for sale in Portland").
2. **Informational queries:** this is a user wanting to learn more about a topic, place, or product (e.g., "Things to do in Portland").
3. **Navigational queries:** this is a user trying to find an online target (e.g., "Portland Timbers official page").

Imagine you own a shop that sells mobile phones. If your keyword analysis shows that users search for both "cell phone" and "mobile phone," using both keywords in your copy is the best way to attract all users. As long as the content makes sense and reads well, this strategy is great. The worst thing you can do is ignore one of the keywords altogether! Not all of your audience will use the same keywords to find your business, so it's crucial that you cater to as many variants as possible.

I mentioned earlier that search engines crawl through the web looking for the most relevant results for your search. The crawlers—also called robots or spiders—are automated. You can help them find the content they're looking for on your website. One way to do this is to provide them with a good website link structure. The robots need a clear route to all of your pages in order to decide if your website is the one the user is looking for.

Imagine you have friends visiting from out of town, and they don't have GPS. As well as your address, you would give them tips on the fastest route across town and landmarks to look out for. This is what you're doing for the search engine robots.

You may want to speak to your web developer to make sure they've mapped out a clear route to your website.

3 Roadblocks That Can Obstruct Search Engine Crawlers

1. Content that's hidden behind login screens and other online forms.
2. Content that's in a rich media format, including text in Flash files.
3. Errors in a website's crawling commands within the HTML code.

The Power of Keywords

DO YOU KNOW how search engines like Google work? The instant you type anything into Google's search engine, Google searches through massive databases of websites out there to find out what would be the best and most relevant results for you. Websites that provide high-quality information about the subject you're looking for will show up at the top, while unrelated, spammy, or malicious sites sink to the bottom.

Your goal as a website owner is to make sure your websites rank at the very top of all the keywords you want to be found for. If you're a carpenter in New York, you want your website as close to the top of the page as possible for the keywords "Best Carpenter New York."

Remember, you need to know what your audience is searching for, but you also need to know the demand for this keyword or phrase. Some keywords are popular (e.g., "best restaurant"), while others are more targeted (e.g., "best indian restaurant Vancouver Broadway"). You need to decide what keywords to concentrate your attention on.

At the end of the day, driving visitors to your website doesn't make it a success. You want to get the right people there, the ones who are most likely to buy, telephone, sign up for, or otherwise answer your call to action. So begin by looking at the kinds of keywords that are of value to you.

Long-Tail versus Short-Tail Keywords

LONG-TAIL KEYWORDS ARE words or phrases that aren't typed very often, and, therefore, won't drive tons of traffic to your website. For example, "Nike new basketball shoes cheap" is much more specific and targeted than "basketball shoes." They're usually relatively long (three to six words) and specific. They can, thus, generate a high conversion rate.

Short-tail keywords are words or phrases that are typed most often, such as "sneakers" or "baking." They can be large drivers of traffic if your website ranks highly on that particular keyword. These keywords or phrases are relatively short (one to two words) and can be competitive or difficult to rank highly with.

One easy mistake to make as a marketer is to aim straight for the short-tail keywords, because they have the most traffic opportunities. Yes, these are the most common keywords in your market, but they still only consist of less than 30 percent of all web searches. The other 70 percent of searches involve long-tail keywords and phrases.

Let's go back to Fred's Bakery in Vancouver. Fred's website is currently targeting short-tail keywords, such as "bakery," "cakes," and "birthday cakes." He's getting a lot of visitors to his website, but doesn't understand why so few of them call to order cakes. He has a great-looking website—which customers always compliment him on—but he's struggling to gain new online customers. What should he do?

From a keyword point of view, the answer is simple: Fred needs to improve his keyword targeting to include exactly what his bakery sells and provides.

What Fred doesn't realize is that many of his visitors are people searching for "cakes" in general. Some are looking for inspiration as they cook; others want a picture of a cake for a

3 Reasons for Targeting Long-Tail Keywords

1. They generally convert traffic better than short-tail keywords.
2. The searches are more specific, so the user who reaches your website knows exactly what they're looking for.
3. You can double-up on your keyword targeting and reach users searching with both long- and short-tail keywords.

school project or a recipe for cupcakes. It's time Fred tailored his keywords to target people searching for his precise services.

Fred does a keyword analysis and finds that he's better off chasing the long-tail keywords, such as "bakery shops in Vancouver," and "custom birthday cakes for sale." These keywords are more relevant to Fred's location and the service he provides. They also include the short-tail keywords he was using before.

So Fred and his web developer change his keywords and phrases. His website traffic goes down a little, but he's getting more orders and calls than ever before because his keywords are more valuable to his business.

3 Online Keyword Tools

IF YOU DON'T have a search engine marketer to analyze your current keywords or create a brand new set, the following tools will help you get started:

1. Google AdWords Keyword Tool
2. Google Trends Keyword Prediction
3. Wordtracker Basic Keyword Demand

There are many tools on the market to help you with your keyword selection. The ones above are all free, but we always recommend starting with the Google tools. These have two great features: they estimate search volumes and tell you the competition targeting each keyword. Both features will help you determine whether or not it's worth targeting a particular phrase.

Building Links to Your Website

THIS SECTION OUTLINES ways in which you can increase inbound and outbound links to your website. Note, not all of these practices will be solutions to your business or market.

However, there will be something for each business or market to use.

How Link-Building Works

WHEN SEARCH ENGINES first came into being, they would tally up the number of links to and from your website to determine how important you were. Spammers found ways to fake this, so the search engines created more sophisticated algorithms that ignore low-quality links and other clutter. They also, now, reward sites that not only have good content but also relevant links back to credible sources.

A link-building campaign will make your website well-liked within your market. It's basically a high school popularity contest; if you're the most liked kid in class, people will want to be associated with you. Linking your website creates a network of trusted online friends who are happy to promote you.

11 Ways to Build Good Links

1. **Post guest blogs.** Invite trusted bloggers to guest post on your articles, or seek opportunities to guest post on other people's articles and blogs, and leave a link to your site. However, keep in mind Google has become much more strict with guest blogging. If someone posts a blog that adds poor-quality content

4 Things to Consider Before Building Your Link Campaign

1. Who will link to your website?
2. Are you organized? Link-building requires continual optimization.
3. Where's your audience online?
4. Remember, content is king—how good is the meat and potatoes of your website? (Apologies to vegans.)

or is obviously just there to build links, Google will severely punish both of your sites. Make sure to only invite high-quality writers and bloggers to contribute to your site.

2. **Create partnerships.** Use loyal customers or partners within the online community to your advantage, and offer them a logo badge and link directing traffic to your website.

3. **Create press releases.** Use free and paid wires to distribute press releases (e.g., prlog.org, marketwire.com, and pitchengine .com).

4. **Sign up with local directory services.** These aren't as essential as they used to be, though it's always worth including your business on Google, Bing, and Yahoo local. Always use an address for local listings, as the search engines determine your importance and relevance based on whether you have a brick-and-mortar shop. Google uses localeze.com to check addresses, so registering there helps too.

5. **Sign up with national directories.** The same applies here as with local directories. Google uses dmoz.org to determine brick-and-mortar, so signing up will always help your ranking. Becoming affiliated with trade bodies within your industry will also add gravitas to your Google position. Ten directory sites are usually all you need to be on.

6. **Link to social media.** A search engine's algorithm will always act favorably toward those websites that have up-to-date LinkedIn, Facebook, and Twitter accounts.

7. **Write testimonials.** Write testimonial pieces for others, while including links to your website. Make sure the testimonial itself is genuine, or it may come off as advertising or blatant self-promotion in poor taste.

8. **Share articles.** Write original articles or re-post blog articles on ezinearticles.com and suite101.com. These sites make your articles more searchable for a user and can increase traffic to your site with a link.

9. **Link to reporter websites.** Using sites such as helpareporter .com can help get your editorial distributed to the masses. This site is home to reporters who need help writing an article. You submit your piece, and they decide if they would like to use it.

10. **Pitch bloggers for product reviews and interviews.** Find reputable bloggers and offer them giveaways and free prizes. The blogger will then write about your product or service, creating more links to your website.

11. **Post on job websites.** Some job sites allow you to post articles about the market your business is in.

12 Things to Consider When Link-Building

The site…
- Is it relevant?
- Are there real people there?
- Is the content well written?
- Is the content updated frequently?

The site's online presence…
- Does the site link out to other sites?
- Does it have good inbound links?
- Is it well established?
- Does it perform well on keyword searches?

The site's policies…
- Are they easy to contact?
- Do they publish resources or reviews?
- Do they invite articles or guest posts?
- Do they interview people for opinion or case studies?

Building Your URL

THE URLS FOR your website and pages aren't just addresses to their online location. They're also a chance to tell your users and the search engines who you are in a brief, effective manner.

For example, Fred's Premium Bakery has been making great cupcakes, birthday cakes, and wedding cakes for ten years. Now, they're finally launching a website to advertise the business and generate sales online. What should Fred's URL be?

Fred's Premium Bakery is a long name. Fred is worried that it's too long for a URL—and most people just call it Fred's Bakery these days, anyways. So instead of using "fredspremiumbakery" as his URL, he decides to go with the shorter "fredsbakery."

Whenever possible, you should use a short, precise phrase that clearly describes your business. Short URLs are easier to copy and paste, are more visible in search listings, and are also easier to remember.

Try creating a URL by combining your most effective keywords with your business name. However, if this doesn't make sense, or the result is unreadable or stuffed with keywords, both users and search engines will go elsewhere. Here, for example, are our page URL names for Fred's Bakery:

www.FredsBakery.com/Cupcakes

www.FredsBakery.com/Birthday-Cakes

www.FredsBakery.com/Wedding-Cakes

The examples above have the name of the business, plus the three top keywords that generate traffic to Fred's website. If Fred has his pages optimized, he will have also used the keyword "cupcake" throughout his Cupcake page. This will create a consistent message throughout his pages, starting with the URL.

Finally, if you want to separate words, make sure to use a hyphen (-), for example: "Birthday-Cakes," not "birthdaycakes." Search engines pick these up much more effectively, and readers will find the URL cleaner and easier to read and remember.

Title and Description Tags: Your Shop Window

TITLE AND DESCRIPTION tags are often forgotten once new websites have been built, when, in fact, they should be high on the SEO priority list. Imagine you are shopping on a street and you see a store window with a fantastic display that includes all the things you need at that exact moment. Title tags are just like that window display: they are the first piece of text a search engine reads. It uses them to determine a web page's subject quickly, so it's important to include the top keywords in a concise manner in the title tags. The title tags should

- be near the top of the HTML script for the search engines to read;
- be different on each web page to reflect the content on show; and
- include the important keywords.

Description tags serve a slightly different purpose, but are just as important. This tag is the piece of text you see in the search listings next to the website's URL. Use your description tag to sell your company to the user. This is an opportunity for you to describe your products or services in a short space. It could be the difference between someone visiting your website or your closest competitor's site instead. So spend some time getting this right.

Designing and Developing Your Website with SEO

ONCE YOU HAVE your top three to five keywords, use them in the title tag at least once, as close to the beginning as possible. The search engines will deem this keyword more important. The top keywords should be used near the top of the web page—in a relevant and constructive place, of course. Use these same keywords twice more in the body copy of the web page. Balance this with the amount of text on the page, and ensure the copy makes sense. When in doubt, choose readability over keyword repetition. Make sure these same keywords are inserted into any images on your page. This helps rankings in Google Images and other non-Google online searches. Make sure your page URL incorporates the same top keywords.

What *Not* to Do in SEO

THE SOPHISTICATED, NEW algorithms that search engines use punish those who try to scam them. You may only be doing it inadvertently, but be careful: if you try to "trick" the search engines into thinking you're a relevant website or bend the rules for gain, the consequences could seriously damage your business. There are three major web no-nos that can cause you penalties.

One is keyword stuffing. Chances are you've seen web pages that not only make little sense but also look "spammy." They're probably packed full of the same keywords repeatedly. Search engines won't reward you for stuffing the same keywords over and over on a web page. They're intelligent enough to know what makes sense and what doesn't, so play it safe, and always make sure the content makes sense to the reader.

Another is link spamming and manipulating. These are probably the most common forms of bad practice. They come in many varieties, but all businesses should be careful not to link to websites that are set up purely for the use of links. Search engines can and will pick up on this. Don't buy links from websites and networks. Not only does this manipulate the search engines, but also the traffic coming back from these links probably won't be interested in your content anyway.

And the third is cloaking. Always make sure the information a search engine can read is the same as the information the reader sees. If the HTML code has different keywords or discusses a different topic than the one on the page, search engines won't rank you highly. This bad practice is called cloaking.

If you employ an SEO consultant to create a strategy or look after your SEO, make sure you ask them what techniques they'll be using. However tempting it may seem, you must avoid falling into one of the traps above. Always be clear what techniques your consultants are using at all times in order to avoid them.

· 5 ·

Social Media

SOCIAL MEDIA IS an umbrella term for media created or shared through online networks. The biggest difference between social media and just putting messages up on your website is the whole user interaction element.

In the past, companies would write updates on their pages and people would come, absorb the information, and then leave. Now it's very much a two-way conversation. Companies and audiences can interact through commenting, liking, and sharing, and businesses now have a chance to build brand loyalty, push promotions, and communicate with their customers more than ever before.

Unfortunately, many businesspeople still view social media as a gimmick—one that might stick around but has no meaningful business value. Like it or not, social media is now an essential part of operating a business. You can't just build a website and blog, and then expect people to embrace your brand. You need to engage your customers and your clients—the ones who love you and the ones who hate you.

Although there are now many hundreds of social media networks, some businesses are still reluctant to get involved in social networking. A lot of executives might know they need social media—mainly because it's in the news and all their competitors are doing it—but they have no idea how to do it or why it'll actually benefit their business.

Meanwhile, traditional forms of media are shrinking, and social networking and online media are growing at phenomenal rates in all demographics. Because social media creates "virtual word-of-mouth" publicity, it can be a very powerful and effective tool, especially for local businesses that rely on reputation and recommendations.

The Value of Social Media for Small Business

TRADITIONAL MEDIA USES a broadcast model, where communication is a one-way street from one source to many passive consumers. Social media flips this model on its head by turning everyone into content creators who can comment and post materials online. This allows conversation to occur where previously there was only broadcasting. This has been a huge change for major companies, which must now personally address their customers in a public space.

Social media goes beyond trendiness—it represents a fundamental change in the way we communicate and look for information. People born after 1992 can't remember a world before the Internet. They don't read newspapers, and they barely read magazines or watch TV—they're digital natives, born and bred online.

Social media allows customers to actively and openly discuss their experiences with products, companies, and brands and to share their recommendations with more than just their immediate social circle.

It's more than likely that people are talking about your

brand right now. Since social media platforms permit companies to take part in the conversations that consumers are having about them, companies are now able to manage their messaging and learn what their customers are seeking.

Social media is an entire arena in which companies must establish a presence. Trend reports show more and more people use the Internet every day as a tool for finding information on recommended products and services, so your target market is already heavily involved online and they use the web to discover and research their next purchase.

5 Things Social Media Can Do for Your Business

SOCIAL MEDIA HAS become the most cost-effective marketing tool out there, and if you're not going to take advantage of it, your competitors will.

If done correctly, social media can help you with the following:

1. **Attract new clients** by creating a greater presence for your company online, so you increase the likeliness of an individual coming across it. Customers who have enjoyed your products and services can also share your content with their friends and social circles, giving your brand much greater reach.

   Different social media platforms will have different audiences, so understanding your target demographic is key to actually reaching it. It's also important to know which social media platforms to focus on; you don't need to be on every single social platform.

2. **Strengthen bonds with existing clients.** Social media is all about making personal connections. A customer who is constantly given information and updates about a business is more likely to be loyal. Because your customer is seeing your brand

more frequently through social media, your company is more likely to remain top-of-mind when the customer is making a purchase decision in the future.

3. **Build your brand.** Branding used to be a very expensive proposition. You would have to invest thousands of dollars in marketing and publicity to reach your audience frequently and gain status as an expert in your field. Social media allows you to garner this kind of attention and create articles positioning yourself as an expert at a fraction of the cost. Although social media (Facebook in particular) is becoming more expensive as it reaches critical mass, it's still the most inexpensive option compared to other forms of advertising.

4. **Invest in search engine optimization (SEO).** Google has effectively become the new Yellow Pages. Turning up in the first results of Google is one of the single most beneficial things that can happen for your business, and social media can help this happen. For more information about SEO, look at chapter 4.

5. **Research and learn about your target market.** Social media sites encourage users to post their hobbies and passions. This allows businesses to learn more about their customers. Personal information has become harder to access through numerous privacy scandals, but you should still be able to get a good idea about a person's interests and habits from the types of things they talk about on social media.

If you are new to social media and are worried about not getting it quite right or, worse, being called a troll (the worst kind of people on social media, who only want to offend and attack instead of engage in positive dialogue), here are a few easy rules to follow.

1. **Create valuable content.** Customers need to be given a *reason* to visit a blog or Facebook page regularly, or to follow you on Twitter. It's not enough to hope that people will join simply because they like your business.

This reason must be content.

Your social media networks need to be publishing and distributing information that's interesting, valuable, and informative. Whatever posts you write or content you create needs to stand out from hundreds—or even thousands—of others.

2. **Offer incentives.** One of the fastest ways to grow a social media following is to offer contests. By using Facebook, Twitter, and local bloggers, you can set up contests that require that individuals become fans or followers in order to win prizes. Not only does this allow you to grow your fan base, it's also extremely beneficial to your business's online brand, as social media users—particularly Twitter users—look very favorably upon organizations that offer contests.

3. **Enter the conversation.** To be truly successful in social media, one must form connections, engage with fans, and present a personality the public can relate to. The best way to do this is to assign one person from your company to look after social media and monitor social media alerts (Google Alerts), so they can join in the conversation no matter where it occurs.

   Remember, the person you choose to run your social media presence will be your brand ambassador to the entire online world, so it's not a position to be taken lightly.

4. **Create calls to action.** It should be very easy for visitors to use your site to find the information they want. Ensure any promotions or events are clearly advertised on your home page. Your home page (and subsequent pages, if possible) should always have a link to a contact form or your "Contact Us" page, so people can easily get in touch for more information.

Which Social Media Platform Should I Target?

THE FIRST STEP is research. Find out which sites, forums, and online groups relate to you. A breakdown of some of the biggest and most widely used social networks follows, but there are many more springing up every week. Use this guide as a rough cheat sheet of what each social media network has to offer you and your business. Not every social media service is the right fit for your company. For example, an industrial company will find themselves very isolated on Tumblr or Instagram.

Facebook

FACEBOOK ALLOWS YOU to create a profile page to represent yourself or your business. The page contains basic information, such as what city you live in, where you work, and where you went to school, and it may contain photos that you or your followers have added. With over a billion visitors per month, Facebook is the largest social network in the world. It's ideal for marketing once you have everything in place and people want to engage with you and your products or services. Fan pages, wall posts, applications, and social ads make it a popular choice for both companies and customers.

Pros: You can define your target audience by a number of targeting parameters. Your ads have the outreach of a TV ad and the precision of direct marketing, all within the frame of trusted connections. Anyone who wants to find you on Facebook easily can, and, if they wish, they can share your company with all their friends.

You can also promote offers using Facebook advertising. People can click the ad to receive a special coupon in their email to take to your store. This directly ties online engagement with physical sales and foot traffic.

Cons: Facebook is increasingly becoming a pay-to-play social media network. Many posts will only reach a fraction of your fans—unless you pay for advertising—with organic reach and engagement severely dropping for companies across the board. Even paid ads are becoming less and less effective as adblock, a browser plug-in that blocks Internet advertisements, becomes more prevalent and competition increases.

Twitter

TWITTER IS BEST described as a micro-blogging site. Like a blog, it allows you to publish content; however, it limits you to doing so in 140-character fragments. Individuals who have decided they're interested in receiving your updates (followers) will see your content when they log into the site.

Pros: You can keep your company in the mind of customers through short posts every day. You can post relevant, helpful content to establish yourself as an industry leader, direct traffic to your new content (blogs, infographics, etc.), and even directly handle customer service requests. Photos can also be attached to tweets to increase the visibility of your tweets.

Cons: You have to keep your message short, because only 140 characters are allowed for one post.

LinkedIn

LINKEDIN IS A social network for companies and business professionals. It's a valuable tool for making new business contacts and keeping in touch with former co-workers and clients.

LinkedIn members can create customizable profiles with details of their career (employment history, business accomplishments, and other professional achievements). LinkedIn is a network specifically created for professionals that allows users to connect with colleagues and share information and opportunities. Networking with other local businesses is a great way to raise your profile and learn about new collaborative opportunities.

Pros: LinkedIn is an ideal platform for connecting with business contacts. There's a great deal of interesting content posted by users that's business-related and that can help your business grow.

Cons: After setting up your profile, filling in the details of your career, and connecting with former co-workers, there's no obvious way to update your presence. You've got to work at it; just don't let it become a people-collector site rather than a social media and new business tool.

Google+

GOOGLE+ IS OFTEN referred to as a social media graveyard. This social network definitely has a smaller share of the market compared to Facebook and Twitter, but it shouldn't be overlooked. Google+ is small, but we've found that the level of engagement and traffic are often of much higher quality than those of other sites, like Facebook or Twitter.

Pros: Google+ can help you organize your followers and pinpoint your targeting using Google+ Circles. This can help you tailor your content to your followers to gain the maximum impact. Since Google+ is closely tied to Google's search engine, favourable Google+ content will also be well-reflected in your SEO efforts.

Cons: When all is said and done, Google+ just has a much smaller audience than other social media sites. Your time may be better spent on other channels, like Facebook, Twitter, or LinkedIn, if you already have a large following on those sites.

WordPress

AS YOU NOW have read, WordPress is an open-source content management system (CMS) that's highly flexible. It's often used as a blog publishing application powered by PHP and MySQL. It has many features, including a plug-in architecture and template system. WordPress is one of the most popular CMSs in use today.

WordPress is a good platform for small businesses looking for an affordable way to create a website without starting from scratch. See Appendix 1 for details on how to use it to build your website.

Pros: It's very easy to develop a WordPress website, especially because many themes can be simply plugged in with the click of a button. Updating content is also very simple, because WordPress has a huge amount of tools, applications, and other products to utilize.

Cons: There's not much freedom in user management. It's not that easy to include your own design, because much of the WordPress code isn't where you would expect it. Since WordPress began as blogging software, it doesn't cope well with too many individual pages.

Pinterest

PINTEREST IS MEANT to connect people through shared interests. It's an innovative, online pinboard where so-called Pinners collect and share images and videos they find on the web. Images, or Pins, may be organized into Pinboards, which can then be customized, themed, and followed by other users. As on Facebook, users also like or re-pin content shared by other Pinners.

Pros: Pinterest differs from many other social media platforms in that it's image-based, which has allowed it to find a following among those with interests that have a strong visual component. This is why Pinterest is popular for sharing recipes, interior design, fashion, and online shopping. Each of these pins can also be used as an advertisement. Many clothing stores photograph and post all of their inventory onto Pinterest, taking users straight to the corresponding e-commerce page when clicked.

Cons: While Pinterest is great for creative and visual companies, such as interior designer firms, the Pinboards of other companies look more like product catalogues than a social experience. Another big issue is the copyright question Pinterest continues to face. Whenever you pin something, *make sure you have the image rights*. There have been stories of people being fined over $8,000 for using a $10 copyright image without paying.

YouTube

YOUTUBE HAS GROWN from a small video-sharing site to the definitive video entertainment website of the world. Anyone can upload a movie about almost anything they want—unless it's copyrighted—and many singers, actors, and musicians have jump-started their careers by becoming popular through YouTube.

Businesses, however, are finding that YouTube is an incredible resource. Commercials can be shared and advertised through YouTube for a fraction of the price of TV advertising, and calls to action can be embedded straight into the video itself. Best of all, popular video clips can even be monetized with ads, acting as an additional revenue stream for your business.

If you have engaging branded content, YouTube is a powerful marketing platform where you can upload an unlimited number of clips and customize your own channel. Pay attention to building relationships with subscribers and users; don't just treat it as a push channel.

Pros: YouTube provides fast, easy video-sharing features. It has good privacy features, and users can easily comment on clips. Calls to action can be added to videos to direct traffic to websites and landing pages. YouTube advertising is also very effective, and only charges you if someone watches the full ad. YouTube also allows you to do minor visual edits on your video.

Cons: Many YouTube features, such as commenting, are now tied directly to your Google+ account. Make sure you have a robust Google+ account before starting. YouTube is also very stringent on copyright infringement. Be very careful about the music you upload, because your account can be flagged and shut down if you have too many infractions. While YouTube used to have many restrictions, they've added many features to help video creators.

Tumblr

TUMBLR IS A woefully underrepresented social media platform when it comes to marketing businesses. Everyone has a Facebook and Twitter account, but not very many businesses ever look twice at Tumblr.

For those who don't know, Tumblr is a huge community of image blogs. Users post images or animated GIFs to their group of followers, who can, in turn, share them to their followers. Structure-wise it's similar to Twitter, but much more image-friendly. Conversely, traditional blog posts—especially ones with no pictures or media—generally don't do as well.

Tumblr works best for visual industries. The culture of Tumblr is incredibly receptive to photos and videos. However, you can upload music and plain text as well.

Pros: One of Tumblr's strongest features is that animated GIFs are popular and common. By animating your photos or converting your videos into bite-sized clips, you can get a lot of attention.

One of Tumblr's advantages is that it's very easy to share material found on it, also known as reblogging. Everyone is constantly reblogging things to their friends, and, as a result, they're constantly on the lookout for good content. For you, that means a crowd of followers that will excitedly share any posts they like to their networks. Some posts will be shared over several hundred thousand times!

Scheduling posts is a built-in feature for Tumblr. You can easily create a queue and spread your content over the next couple of weeks. It may be tempting to just repurpose your Facebook or Twitter feed for Tumblr, but try to spice it up a bit with animated images or even videos whenever you can.

Cons: According to Alexa (a commercial web traffic data provider—kind of like the Neilsen ratings, which measure TV audiences), Tumblr is mostly inhabited by high school- and university-aged females. This isn't necessarily a downside, but it's something to be aware of when deciding what kinds of content to post. Although there's content for everybody on Tumblr, there's a heavy skew toward film, fashion, art, and animals.

From personal experience, Tumblr's user base can only be described as fickle. Many users don't want to see businesses on their Tumblr dashboards, and they'll go to extra lengths not to be associated with businesses. Extra care must be taken to make both your account and your content less business-like and more casual.

Yelp

YELP IS A review site where members post their reviews and opinions of restaurants, hotels, businesses, parks, beaches, and anything else they see fit to review. If you're a retail business or restaurant, you need to be on Yelp and make sure you have a solid rating in order to drive new business.

Pros: A good review score on Yelp can make your business. You can bet new customers will check your reviews on Yelp before actually dropping in, even if they were initially referred by friends. Customers can also get a lot of information about your business, including location, business hours, restaurant type, parking information, and so on.

Cons: Anybody can review your business, including your competitor. People are more likely to post bad reviews than good ones, so you have to pay attention to your site and your business to keep it positive.

A negative Yelp score can be seriously detrimental to your customer inflow, so it's crucial that you watch your scores like a hawk. If people point out a flaw—cold food, poor service, dirty kitchenware—go back into your restaurant and make sure the problem is fixed as soon as possible. *Ignoring negative reviews won't make them go away.*

Social Bookmarking Sites

SOCIAL BOOKMARKING SITES operate like the bookmark function in your web browser, where you flag a page that you like and want to return to. Social bookmarking makes this list public, so individuals can share with like-minded individuals the interesting, funny, or educational websites they find. Social bookmarking sites are good for businesses because they show what subjects are currently trending on the Internet. Studies have also shown that social bookmarking has a positive effect on a website's search ranking.

6 Great Social Bookmarking Sites

StumbleUpon

Digg

Delicious
Fark
DZone
Newsvine

Using a Facebook Page for Your Business

WHILE YOU PROBABLY already have a Facebook profile for yourself or your business, having a Facebook page for your business is much better. Make the change and you'll improve your Facebook presence in no time.

4 Advantages of Facebook Pages

1. People can "like" your Facebook page without you having to confirm it. This is in contrast to profiles, where you have to confirm each individual friend request.
2. A Facebook page allows users to schedule posts.
3. A Facebook page also allows a business to pay for premium placement of posts known as "promoted posts." You can greatly increase the visibility of your posts by having them show up for a specific, targeted audience.
4. A Facebook page has better functionality than a profile. For example, it allows you to assign different administrative roles to different people in your business. It also allows you to pin and highlight posts to the top of your page, and it gives you access to powerful analytical tools.

For step-by-step instructions on how to set up a Facebook page for your business, read Appendix 2.

Building up Your Media Authenticity

AUTHENTICITY IS ONE of the biggest issues facing business pages on Facebook right now. Here's the problem: people don't like seeing ads. If you're trying to use your Facebook page to do nothing but sell a product or service, you're in for a bad time. Unlike other forms of marketing, like radio or TV commercials, Facebook gives users the ability to hide content they don't like seeing with a single click.

To succeed at Facebook marketing, you need to provide content that people actually want to see rather than offer them only what you want to say. As a business, it's very tempting to tie every single post you make back to your products, but, for many people, that's a major turn-off.

Your Facebook page *isn't* an advertising platform, it's a brand-building platform. Use your page to interact and engage with your followers, not milk them for profits.

Why Awareness Just Isn't Enough

PERHAPS YOU'VE READ through and tried your luck with Facebook ads, and managed to get yourself 100 likes or so. You put out new content every now and then, but only a handful of people see it, much less interact with it. What do you do?

At this point, many people would talk about raising awareness. When it comes to traditional media, like TV and radio, awareness might be a suitable benchmark, but social media is a completely different channel. You can and should look beyond awareness and start focusing on engagement.

Don't get me wrong, awareness is definitely important, but, as a business, you can't let that be your one and only goal.

Why Is Engagement So Important?

FACEBOOK GIVES COMPANIES so many tools to talk to and message their fans directly. They can build relationships, tailor individual campaigns, and craft their brand image in ways companies never could a decade ago. Having a solid community of engaged individuals behind your Facebook brand is one of the biggest goals and challenges of Facebook marketing.

Don't believe me? Here are three big benefits of having a close-knit community.

1. **High engagement builds up brand champions.** If someone likes your company enough to actively like, comment on, and share your page, they're most likely very engaged with your brand. These people are what we would consider "brand champions:" people who are in love with your brand and what it stands for. A brand champion is someone who voluntarily shares your content, brand messaging, and company vision. They don't just promote you during a campaign, they promote you all the time.

2. **Engaged users protect against negative publicity.** No one knows exactly when a crisis will hit your company. Snapchat didn't. American Airlines didn't. You probably won't either. As a result, it's important to have a loyal foundation of followers who will defend your actions and ease the pressure off your company.

    Obviously this doesn't give your company free rein to do unethical or illegal acts, but having the community on your side could spell the difference between a well-intentioned company that made a mistake, and a greedy pack of liars that deserved everything they got.

3. **More brand loyalty means more profit.** I understand that profits are important. I own a business too. Here's the big question I'm sure is on everyone's mind: *are brand champions more important than customers?*

    To be honest, the two really aren't mutually exclusive. If someone is truly a brand champion and cares about your company and products, they'll probably already be a customer. On the path toward obtaining brand champions, you'll obtain customers.

At the end of the day, businesses need to make money, and Facebook is ultimately a means to that end. Cultivating relationships with potential customers on Facebook will change them into long-term customers who are more likely to stick with you even through price increases.

So what's the problem? It's obvious that having highly engaged individuals is great, but it's *much* harder than it looks to actually convert regular followers into loyal brand champions. If it were easy, every company that used Facebook would have an army of profit-generating brand champions. Why is it so difficult? There are three major roadblocks that prevent many companies from ever building long-lasting relationships with their customers.

First, people don't care about you, they care about themselves. This is a major stumbling block for many businesses unfamiliar with Facebook. Companies often post exclusively about themselves, their products, or their promotions. If you come from an advertising background, this concept may seem foreign to you. Instead of focusing on you, use your brand page to talk to and interact with your community. A few posts a week discussing the news or having a casual conversation will go a long way to build brand loyalty.

Before I go any further, I need to draw a distinction. Using actual Facebook ads is fine. The purpose of these is to get people to like your page or your website, and is very similar to traditional advertising. However, at Curve we strongly advise against using actual Facebook posts to constantly sell your products. A post every now and then is fine, but you need to focus on engaging your audience.

Second, people generally assume you're just trying to make money off them. Do you actually care about your customers, or are you just trying to squeeze them for a quick buck? Your business needs to focus on the value you can bring to your customers. What benefit do they get for paying attention to your page? Is it entertaining or thought-provoking?

If every single post you make is desperately trying to push a sale or a promotion, people will start ignoring you. You need to be *interesting* to people, or they'll completely tune you out. Remember, a company that only talks about itself will soon find itself completely alone.

Third, your business is one voice out of millions. Your posts, photos, and stories are in direct competition with every other page, friend, or story that shows up on your followers' news feed. Even on the off chance that someone sees your post, there's still a good chance they'll ignore it or, worse yet, unfollow you.

Unlike TV or radio audiences, Facebook individuals have a lot of power when it comes to what they do or don't want to see. If they think your content is subpar or irrelevant, they can remove you with a single click.

We've talked about using paid advertising to bring in some likes for your page. Now that your page has its own group of followers, you should examine organic methods to communicate with them. Here are a few examples:

1. Convert followers into brand champions.
2. Make good use of holiday marketing.
3. Respond properly to negative criticism.
4. Use contests and promotions on Facebook.

How to Transform Your Followers into Brand Champions

A BRAND CHAMPION is an individual who's so loyal to your brand and your business that they'll happily tell all their friends and family about you.

Growing these followers will play a significant role in the long-term success of virtually any business. Unfortunately, only a tiny fraction of a business's follower base will interact with you, much less be considered a brand champion.

There's no beating around the bush here. Talking and interacting with fans on a one-on-one basis can be a time-consuming process, especially for larger companies. We suggest starting out small. Message one or two of the most highly engaged followers, and try to communicate with them. We're not saying this is the only way to get brand champions, but build up your network of strong, engaged followers, one champion at a time, and soon you'll have a huge network of loyal champions.

Here are three quick steps for engaging with the followers you have and (hopefully!) nurture them into becoming champions for your cause.

1. **Identify your fans.** The first step is to figure out who your real fans are! Look through the last thirty days on your Facebook page. Who has liked your posts the most? Who has shared and commented? Throw the data into an Excel file, and find out if there are any potential candidates waiting to be picked up. With any luck, your graph will look a little something like this.

The chart shows a small number of fans are contributing a larger-than-average proportion of likes.

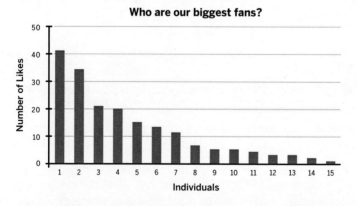

Engagement levels of our biggest fans

On Twitter, you can see how many people retweet, mention, or favorite your posts. Try to find people who consistently engage with your content. If engagement levels are low, it may be time to re-evaluate your tweets.

2. **Personally contact the most engaged fans.** Take the time to send your fans a personalized private message. Don't copy and paste the same message for every person. Try to tailor it for each individual as best you can. Many people ignore messages from businesses, because they assume they're trying to sell them something. Be authentic and genuine in your message, and thank them for liking your content.

   If it's in your budget, a small gift as a token of your appreciation can go a long way toward making people like you. A personal gift shows that your intentions are genuine, and you're not just trying to squeeze a sale out of them. Make sure it's something relevant to your business, like a coupon or product samples.

3. **Tailor a call to action to suit their needs.** After you've established rapport with your key customers, it may be time to add a call to action. The type of call to action will depend on your previous interactions with them. Are they interested in finding more information about buying your product? Are they interested in receiving more information? It's your job to identify and find the right call to action.

   For example, if you have a follower who's very interested in a non-profit initiative your company is doing, ask them to sign up for your newsletter or register for your website for more information about your company's community involvement.

Holiday Marketing and Promotion

WHILE YOU'RE TRYING to move forward and create brand champions one at a time, you need to keep the content and updates on your page constantly rolling in. One great way to do this is to take advantage of the nearest holiday to promote your brand.

Holiday marketing is one of the oldest yet most effective ways to get a response from your audience. The end goal here isn't to post something just because everyone else is doing it, but because it gives you a chance to engage with your followers. To demonstrate different techniques, we'll use Valentine's Day as an example. Note, these can be applied to any holiday.

Remember, try to avoid using plain text posts whenever possible. Web users love visual media, and using videos and photos will build engagements with your fans. Still, if you just don't have the time to find a nice photo, even a simple text post can bring some holiday cheer to your page. It only takes a second, and talking about upcoming events and holidays can help you build a connection with your followers. This is important because it adds authenticity to your brand.

If you already have a sale running, put a holiday spin on it! For example, if you're a company that sells ski equipment, and you already have a February sale—since spring is coming, and people are focusing less on skiing—change it into a Valentine's Day sale to draw more attention to it.

Anyone can post a generic photo of hearts or chocolates, but, if you want to stand out, you should create one from scratch and tie it to your company.

Remember, never just say "Happy Valentine's Day" and leave it at that. Ask your followers about their plans. Talk to them about what they like or dislike the most about the holiday. Use the holiday as a reason to engage with your user base. It might take a bit of thinking or work to post something creative during Valentine's Day—or any other holiday, for that matter—but it's definitely worth the effort. It gives you and your followers a common talking point and opens the door to further engagement and communication.

Responding to Negative Criticism

EVERY COMPANY WILL, at some point, run into negative criticism no matter what, especially in the world of social media. Negative criticism happens to everyone, and how you deal with it is actually more important than the complaint itself. If you're not careful, your response could do irreparable damage to your reputation through poor handling of your critics.

Most proud business owners find it very hard to stay calm at the sight of a negative comment. You may want to become overly defensive or emotional, but you cannot and should not let this happen.

Remember, not everyone who has something negative to say is out to hurt your company. Maybe they've actually been wronged through poor customer service or a defective product.

A good rule of thumb is to give yourself a few minutes to cool down before responding to any criticism. Remember, one angry tweet or post on social media is impossible to retract or delete. It's always best to plan your response and make sure it's free of passive aggressiveness or sarcasm.

The next time you feel the need to have an outburst, follow this little mental exercise. Imagine that a reporter took your response and used it as the headline for every major newspaper in the country, tomorrow morning. Would the article damage your reputation or improve it? Would your boss be pleased with how you handled it or would you be fired?

Contests and Promotions on Facebook

IS YOUR FACEBOOK page looking a little empty? It may be time to use a contest or a promotion to give your brand a boost. Here's why we love using contests and promotions:

1. **Contests give a tangible reason for your fans to get involved with you.** Once people start engaging with your page, you now have a list of individuals who feel strongly about your business. This is a great way to start a conversation with them and start building brand loyalty.

2. **Popular contests can automatically spread your brand's page.** Although it's explicitly against Facebook's regulations to ask your friends to share your promotion post, there's nothing stopping them from doing it on their own. If a contest is very popular, there's a chance that your fans will spread it to their friends as well.

    For many years, Facebook didn't allow promotions on business pages. The rules were confusing and forced many page owners to rely on third-party apps to run any contests or promotions. Thankfully, Facebook has since changed their rules regarding contests and promotions. Nowadays, a business is allowed to run a page promotion, as long as they abide by the following rules.

    - **You're responsible for the entire operation.** You need to make it very clear that Facebook isn't affiliated with your contest, and you and your company are responsible for every single aspect of the operation. This includes legal issues, like age and residency restrictions, any regulations around the prizes being offered, and so on.

    - **Promotions must be done on pages.** Promotions aren't allowed on personal timelines, even if you make it clear that you're doing it on behalf of a company. Facebook brand pages are the only places you're allowed to run a promotion.

    - **Applicants can't share to enter.** No matter what your contest is about, applicants cannot enter it by sharing your post. However, applicants can like or comment on a page post to enter the contest.

Facebook's full list of guidelines can be found at facebook .com/page_guidelines.php. With these new rules, it's important to look at some of the things you are and aren't allowed to do.

Allowed	Not Allowed
Have someone like or comment on a page post to enter.	Require that someone shares a post or a photo to enter.
Use likes as voting mechanism (whichever post gets voted on the most wins).	Require that someone posts something on their personal timeline to enter.
Require that someone messages your page to enter.	Require that someone tags themself in a photo to enter.

Facebook Insights: What Does It Mean and How Can It Help You?

RECENTLY, THE ABILITY to measure social media has become more important, as businesses want to know how effective their tweets and posts really are. One of the key ways to measure the success of all your social media efforts is to look at analytics.

Facebook Analytics—also known as Insights—is a free tool that becomes available once your page has at least thirty likes.

To access your Insights, click on the "Insights" tab between "Activity" and "Settings" on your business page (see next page).

Facebook Insights provides powerful analytics on the behavior of your visitors and the performance of your page. While there's just too much information on analytics to cover in one chapter, I do go into much greater detail in my free Facebook e-book that can be found at curvecommunications.com/landing/facebook-marketing, so refer to that if you need more information.

Here are four burning questions that can be answered using Facebook Insights.

1. **When is the best time to post on Facebook?** One of the best things Facebook provides is information on what time and what day of the week your visitors are most active. Instead of blasting out your content at the same time every week, you can time your articles and status updates to have the most impact.

2. **Which of my posts are most popular?** The "Pages" tab shows detailed statistics for all of your existing posts. This can be useful for three reasons:
   - It shows you the number of people who clicked a link on your post, which isn't available anywhere else;
   - You can easily compare performance across many different posts, which can help identify trends that might be helpful for planning future posts; and
   - Each post is sorted by type, so you can gauge the effectiveness of media posts versus status updates.

3. **What are my competitors doing?** If you want to see what your competitors are doing on social media, you can add their business pages in the "Pages to Watch" section. This allows you to

benchmark your performance against other businesses. On top of tracking the number of likes their page has, you can even see the number of likes, shares, and comments for all their posts.

4. **Who is my target audience?** Facebook actually records key demographic information about your fans and people you reach in the "People" tab. Like the graph below shows, you can see the gender and age breakdown of anyone who likes your page You can also see the city, country, and language of choice for all your fans.

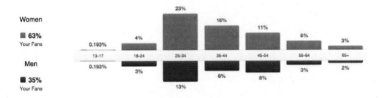

A demographic breakdown of people who "like" your Facebook page.

When Is the Best Time to Post on Facebook?

A WELL-KNOWN THEORY is that half of the total reach of a Facebook post will be achieved in the first thirty minutes. Choosing the correct time to post could greatly impact the number of people who will see it.

Different target audiences will check their phones at different times. For example, if you're targeting high school students, the 3:00 p.m. to 4:00 p.m. segment becomes crucial because they're just getting out of school. If you're targeting young professionals, posts early in the morning are more effective since many of them read the news on their commute.

Here are some of our posting time recommendations:

Time of Day	Reason
8:00 a.m. to 9:00 a.m.	Did you know that 80 percent of people ages 18 to 44 check their phones before they brush their teeth? An early morning post has the potential to be seen by a large number of your followers.
11:00 a.m. to 1:00 p.m.	Both students and employees are on their lunch break.
4:00 p.m. to 6:00 p.m.	Many people check their feeds during dinnertime.

Remember, every business is different. Times that may work for you may not work for your audience.

So when should you post? It might sound like a cop-out answer, but you need to find out for yourself. Test your posts for different times of day, and examine which ones work the best for you. As backward as it may sound, posts that are off peak times may actually end up being more successful, since there's less competition from other pages.

If you just have no idea where to start, try our posting recommendations for one week, and then move the times around for the next week to see if there's any dramatic changes in response or engagement.

This is Constant Contact's advice: "Try to find your engagement sweet-spot by determining the intersection of time when the majority of your audience is on Facebook and the time when the least overall posting is occurring."

Twitter: Micro-blogging Your Business

ANDY BOROWITZ (@BOROWITZREPORT) nicely summarizes the risk of Twitter: "There's a fine line between social marketing and wasting your ******* life." When done incorrectly, Twitter is like a tire in the mud: it spins and spins but gets you nowhere. Unless you have a plan of action, your efforts won't yield any results. However, if you use it correctly, a Twitter account can increase awareness of your business.

Using Twitter for Your Business

UNLIKE FACEBOOK, TWITTER is fast-paced. People are talking to each other constantly, and you need to know what to say and what content to share to get your voice heard above millions of other companies. Here are eleven ways to keep your Twitter account interesting:

1. **Find contacts with similar interests.** If you follow people in the same field as you, there's a good chance they'll follow you back. These people will become a primary source of content that you can retweet. For example, if you're a non-profit organization, follow other popular non-profits and keep track of who's following them. People who are passionate about a certain cause are more likely to follow and retweet posts from a similar cause.

2. **Tell customers, friends, and contacts about your Twitter page.** Send out an email newsletter to all your customers and business contacts, inviting them to follow your Twitter page (make sure to provide a link). Make sure to talk about your Twitter account through your other social media platforms to increase your exposure.

3. **Follow popular Twitter users and news personalities.** If you tweet something that interests a user with a huge following, they may retweet it, and, all of a sudden, your tweet could reach over 50,000 people! You should also follow news personalities

for the same reason. If you're following a popular journalist or reporter from that media outlet you should definitely include them in relevant tweets by simply adding their @name. This will increase the odds of them retweeting you, and get your message across to a much larger group of followers.

Remember, if you put the at-sign (@) at the beginning of your tweet, *only* that user will see the tweet. If you want the tweet to go out to the rest of your followers, put the @ mentions at the end of your tweet instead.

4. **Tweet regularly.** Tweeting once a day isn't enough. You want to be constantly visible on your followers' pages, and, to achieve this, you need to tweet every two to three hours ideally. The best way to do this is to set up a Hootsuite account, which allows you to schedule regular Twitter, Facebook, and WordPress posts. Once a morning, you should come up with six to eight tweets for the day and schedule them at two-hour intervals via Hootsuite or another useful tool I discovered called MeetEdgar.

5. **Finding content to tweet about.** Of course, it can be difficult thinking of half a dozen tweets every single day. Get some help by setting up a Google Alert for keywords that relate to your business. You'll receive an email once a day containing the most recent and relevant news articles linked to your keywords. Additionally, look into content aggregate sites, like Feedly, Alltop, Mashable, and Business 2 Community (depending on your industry). You can use these to find relevant, popular content to tweet about.

Schedule tweets for the articles you think others would like to read, making sure to add the URL (Hootsuite lets you shorten URLs, allowing you more space to describe the articles).

6. **Don't be a robot.** You need to add personality. Not every tweet needs to be an announcement or promotion. You know your customers better than anyone and can probably think of other

things that might interest them. Is there something going on in politics, pop culture, or sports you think they would want to know about?

Furthermore, there's nothing wrong with tweeting content that interests you! It's good to add some personality to your Twitter page, even if that means tweeting about things that have nothing to do with your business.

7. **Thank new followers and engage with them.** When someone new follows you, send out a tweet for all to see (e.g. Thx for @ example1, @example2, and @example3 for following me!). A good idea to save time is to save all of your thanks for one day of the week. You should also engage directly with your followers. Comment on their posts or send them a personal message. This is a great way to develop strong relationships over Twitter. People are far more likely to keep following you if you show them you care enough to send them a message!

8. **Use hashtags, but not too many.** Hashtags (#) are a way for people to find informal discussion groups. For example, creating a tweet with the hashtag #London will create a link that'll redirect you to a list of comments that are all focused on the city of London. Hashtags are a great way to join a conversation and to highlight the focus of your tweet. But don't use them too much—it'll look like you're just trying to get publicity. A good rule of thumb is to stick to two hashtags per tweet.

Spend some time researching popular hashtags before sending your tweet out. Some of our most popular tweets have come from hashtags like #Weird or #LifeTips.

9. **Don't spam people with tweets.** You want your tweets to have substance. Tweeting the same thing ad nauseam (e.g., Buy Now!) is a surefire way to become extremely unpopular on Twitter. People will treat your page as spam, and will only create negative connections with your business and brand.

There's nothing wrong with promoting one of your

products or promotions, but give people some breathing room. Reword the tweet to make it look and feel different, and give yourself a couple of hours to a day leeway to best disseminate your content.

10. **Turn your Twitter page into a helpdesk.** It's great if you can create a theme for your page, like being a reliable source of information on a particular subject. Perhaps you could advertise your Twitter page as a helpdesk (e.g., a fitness center's Twitter page could provide advice on different exercise routines or diets). This helps your Twitter feed stand out by turning it into a customer service tool instead of a loudspeaker for your business.

    This doesn't mean you should only tweet content relating to that theme. What it *does* mean is you should advertise that your Twitter account provides a free service and interacts in discussion groups and trending topics.

11. **Pay attention to trending topics.** On the left-hand side of your Twitter home page is a list of trending topics. You should make a habit of checking out the most popular topics. If the trending topic is relevant to your tweet, then add it into your tweet. This is a way to increase the reach of your tweets.

When Is the Best Time to Tweet?

ACCORDING TO BIT.LY, a link shortening and tracking service, the times listed in the table below are the best and worst times to post on Twitter. However, we recommend doing your own testing using Bit.ly links. Keep track of when your tweets are most popular, and fine-tune the timing of your content to get the most impact.

Best Times to Tweet	Worst Times to Tweet
Tweets posted between 10:00 a.m. and 1:00 p.m. (PST) have the highest average click rates.	Avoid tweeting anytime after 5:00 p.m., especially if your tweet contains a link.
Tweeting earlier in the week is better than later in the week.	Avoid tweeting after 3:00 p.m. on Fridays.
	Avoid the weekends if you want content to go viral.

LinkedIn: The Business Platform

LINKEDIN IS A social business networking site. It allows users to create a professional profile, provide information about their present and past employment, and connect with former and current colleagues. It also lets users link up with customers, vendors, suppliers, and other business contacts.

Company profiles should consist of
- a detailed company description;
- a list of products and services; and
- links to your company website and business pages.

LinkedIn members can follow your company's story. You can even highlight product news and post job offerings. Make sure that you're broadcasting what makes your company unique!

LinkedIn members get the latest news by following your company, so maintaining an informative LinkedIn profile is a great way to engage with your followers and find new employees, customers, or businesses you'd like to work with.

7 Reasons to Invest in LinkedIn

1. **Increase your SEO.** LinkedIn allows you to display your website. This will improve your ranking with Google and other search engines.

2. **Increase your Google PageRank.** LinkedIn allows you to make your profile information available for search engines to index. As Google considers LinkedIn a valuable source, a LinkedIn business page is a good way to influence what people see when they search for you.

3. **Increase your visibility.** The more people who follow your company and the more business contacts you have, the more likely your company will be shown first when someone searches a related product or service. So connect with lots of people and make sure to implement a LinkedIn button, a clickable link, on your website.

4. **Find appropriate experts for job offerings.** LinkedIn has more than 162 million users, most of whom are providing detailed information about their experiences, skills, and expertise, so it's become the number one hiring tool for many companies. Your chances of finding the perfect candidate for your job offering can increase if you include it in your hiring process.

5. **Find business partners.** Many companies provide a business page with detailed information about their products and services, so it's easy to find the perfect business partner for your company by using the search feature.

6. **Use LinkedIn as a communication channel.** If you're preparing a product launch, or you'd like to let your business contacts know about some news, use LinkedIn as a communication channel, and notify your target group by updating your profile. Just like other social media platforms, individuals and companies can post to their followers, driving traffic and increasing engagement.

7. **Establishing yourself and your business as experts.** LinkedIn provides an "Answers" tool. Any LinkedIn user can post a question on any topic. You can demonstrate your expertise in a field by answering these questions.

3 Things You're Doing Wrong with Your Company's LinkedIn Page

1. **Your contact page is missing vital information.** Take some time to look at your company's LinkedIn page. Is your page full of holes and missing information? This makes your company look extremely unprofessional, and gives the impression that your company just doesn't care about their image.

   The only reason someone would look up another company on LinkedIn is if they had some interest in the company. It doesn't matter if they're interested in a job opportunity or a product you sell, or if they just want to know more about your brand, your LinkedIn profile *needs* to be a gateway to your company.

   Take the time to fill out your contact information, company description, and anything else on your profile. Don't let those leads walk away empty-handed!

2. **You use the default connection request.** Don't do this. Remember, every connection you have on LinkedIn is a potential lead. Personalize your invitation and make a strong first impression. They could very well become a client in the future.

Include a personal note: (optional)

I'd like to add you to my professional network on LinkedIn.

- Curve Communications

Just because you remember someone doesn't mean they remember you. Mention your mutual friends, when you met, and why you want to invite them.

Speaking of keeping quality connections...

3. **You have too many useless connections.** Everyone knows someone that has over 800 friends on Facebook. How many friends do you think this person actually has?

The same thing is true of LinkedIn. There's nothing wrong with having a lot of followers, but it's much more important to have followers who actually know and care about your business.

It's tempting to add as many people as possible as a way to grow your network, but, in reality, this just dilutes your leads. It's always better to have a small, concentrated group of followers rather than a large, unconnected group.

Where should I start? If you have no idea what a stand-out company's LinkedIn page looks like, we recommend looking up some of your major competitors. Make sure your site at least looks better than theirs.

Tumblr: For Multimedia Micro-blogging

TUMBLR IS A micro-blogging site that specializes in short, image-heavy content. With almost 65 million accounts, Tumblr is one of the largest, fastest-growing blogging sites on the Internet. It's extremely popular with teens and college-aged people, with half its users under the age of twenty-five.

Tumblr is different than other blogging sites, such as WordPress, in that it's incredibly image- and video-based. In particular, animated GIFs—which are somewhere in between an image and a video—are very popular. Furthermore, Tumblr content is consistently re-posted by other Tumblr users. In this way, Tumblr users interact with each other at a much higher frequency than users of other blog platforms.

Because of this, Tumblr holds a lot of potential for businesses that want to engage in viral marketing. Because of the importance placed on imagery, Tumblr works best for fashion, entertainment, media, animation, automobile, and other image-heavy industries. However, if you can see a way to use attractive visuals that relate to your business, a Tumblr blog is worth considering. For instance, a bakery could use Tumblr to post stunning photos of cupcakes, and a realtor could post attractive lifestyle or design photos based on properties they're currently selling.

When Is the Best Time to Post on Tumblr?

Best Time to Post on Tumblr	Worst Time to Post on Tumblr
The best time is after 7:00 p.m. on average, but especially on Friday evenings.	Possiby due to the young age of the users, posts before 3:00 p.m. are generally poorly received.

Pinterest: For Visuals and Female Fans

PINTEREST IS A social networking platform that provides a virtual pinboard for collecting images. Individuals can "pin" or "like" images that interest them.

Because it has many millions of mostly female visitors, Pinterest offers a high marketing potential. However, as with all social media platforms, it's all about the value you provide to your customers, rather than trying to promote your products.

10 Reasons to Invest in Pinterest

1. **Generate website traffic.** Pinterest is an ideal site to refer traffic to your actual website. To take advantage of it, make sure your content is pinnable by installing a "Pin It" button on your website. Encourage your customers to like and repin your Pinterest content, because the pins themselves can actually link to your content, leading to increased traffic to your website.

2. **Get to know consumer insights.** One of the site's important benefits is the great consumer insight you get through keyword searches. These will help you get to know who your customers are and what they're talking about. You can also check out your competitors and compare how they present their products and services.

3. **Build connections and develop relationships.** Pinterest is all about sharing information, connecting with followers, and building relationships. Create relevant content, and encourage your fans to talk about your products by giving them incentives to do so. For example, you can identify fifty influential Pinterest users and send them a customized gift box based on their pins.

4. **Get inspired.** Pinterest is a great platform for finding inspiration about new product ideas, upcoming trends, and business opportunities. For example, some food businesses use Pinterest to get the latest food decoration ideas.

5. **Find experts.** Some companies also use Pinterest as a hiring platform, since you can connect with experts in various fields (e.g., graphic designers, photographers) and get an impression of their work and portfolio.

6. **Build your brand.** Pinterest is the ideal platform to share your business's point of view, and it can help customers get to know another side of your company. Try to focus on the lifestyle side of your brand, not just on your products and services.

For example, instead of just uploading pictures of its products and services, Fred's Bakery could post pictures of nice cupcakes with the recipe. This helps you build a stronger connection between your customer and your brand.

7. **Promote products and services.** When promoting your products and services on Pinterest, make sure that you're not just advertising them. Combine your brands with lifestyle, and build a nice story around your products.

8. **Use built-in analytics.** Pinterest has an analytics tool that enables you to see how much traffic your website is generating from Pinterest and where on Pinterest it's coming from. Study your analytics before deciding what campaigns are working and what types of people are being drawn to your content. To enable Pinterest analytics, you'll need to upload a piece of code (or a file) to your website for verification.

9. **Run effective competitions.** Pinterest is a great social network for running competitions. Ask local contestants to submit their best photo of something that relates to your business—like a cake, a sailboat, or an example of interior design—for a reward.

10. **Inject your business with personality.** Pinterest is the perfect platform to show off your personality. Use it to show photos and videos of yourself and your co-workers, your work space, and other fun, more personal images.

Pinterest users want to experience lifestyle. They want to get inspired. So make sure you create a pinboard with flair. You can also use Pinterest for sharing your company culture. Invite employees to contribute their ideas. The opportunities on Pinterest are only limited by your imagination. Most Pinterest users are women, so businesses with largely female clientele or that sell visually appealing products should take advantage of this platform.

Instagram: Photo-Sharing for Your Business

INSTAGRAM IS A popular photo-sharing program. This free app was launched in October 2010, and was bought by Facebook two years later for more than $1 billion. It allows users to take pictures, edit them with a number of different filters, and publish them to Instagram or different social media platforms.

How to Use Instagram for Your Business

WITH MILLIONS OF users posting what they like, Instagram has huge business potential. Although the details will depend on the type of business you're running, there are a lot of ways to integrate Instagram into your communications plan. If you're selling products you can showcase, create an account and display pictures of them on Instagram and your other social networking accounts.

Other creative ways of using Instagram as a business include communicating upcoming events, creating a photo contest, telling your company's story with pictures, finding and connecting with people who are interested in your kind of product, and sharing behind-the-scenes pictures. As Instagram is—obviously—very image-oriented, it works best for businesses that are in visual industries. Fashion, makeup, media, photography, transportation, and entertainment all have great synergy with Instagram.

4 Ways to Get the Most Out of Your Instagram Account

1. Connect Instagram with your website, to make it easy for people to connect with you on Facebook or Twitter.
2. Make sure users can like and comment on your pictures. If they do, you could offer to send them additional information about that product.

3. Create searchable hashtags with your pictures so more users can find them through the search feature.
4. Post videos on Instagram (e.g., product presentations, tutorials). The more information users get about your products and services, the more likely they'll be to engage with your company.

YouTube: Why Should Businesses Post Online Videos?

WHEN TRYING TO build your brand online, it's very important to have a wide range of different mediums. Text and images make a good foundation, but online videos have recently become incredibly popular with the dominance of services like YouTube, Vimeo, and Vine.

Videos are valuable because they're easily shareable. Videos that have become popular to the point of being viral have brought in millions—and sometimes billions—of views to companies. Perhaps most importantly, videos allow you to define your brand in a way not possible through basic text and photos.

6 Reasons to Invest Resources into Online Video Marketing

1. **Push your search engine ranking.** The major search engines will pay a lot of attention to online videos, which increases your page rating more than just posting text about a topic. Keywords in the title, description, tags, and even the filename will be picked up and indexed by Google's search crawlers.
2. **Videos are more appealing to customers.** People are more likely to watch a one-minute video about your business than read through a page full of text. Think of it as setting up an Internet commercial. Even better, videos can be used to supplement and support blog posts to give them more impact to clarify your point.

3. **Reach a huge audience.** Video-hosting sites have huge audiences. You can easily reach this target group by uploading engaging videos. If your video is creative and contains relevant content, people will also share it with other users.

4. **It's easy to connect with other social media platforms to boost your marketing profile.** Plenty of users have connected their YouTube account to other social media platforms, which makes it easy to connect with users on other channels, helping to create a holistic online presence.

   YouTube recently changed its structure because it was bought and then combined with Google, making everything a little more interconnected. This crossover of networks will give your videos even more coverage, as they can be easily shared on Google+, as well as YouTube.

5. **Videos never stop working for you.** While your salesperson can only work a few hours a day, your video is making your case 24/7 for free, once it's uploaded. Demonstrate your expertise in your video, and people around the world will continue to see it for weeks and months to come.

6. **Videos give a face to the potential customer.** A video is a very personal way to present your company. The potential customer gets to know you better and experiences your way of doing business.

8 Tips for Making a Great Video

BEFORE YOU START making a video, take some time to think about the basic outline for your film, including a plot and timeline. Your online video should naturally attract potential customers, generate a lead, and convince them to buy your product.

1. **Have a clear, concise message you want to convey with your video.** While your potential customer is watching it, they should feel compelled to learn more about your company and

your products and services. You can measure the success of the video by the number of viewers who then decide to contact you. Inserting click-through annotations and links in the video description can redirect traffic to your website or landing pages. Be sure to make the most of these if you ever decide to use a video!

2. **Consider adding visuals, graphics, or charts,** which can show the viewer how your products and services work or what their benefits are. Make sure all the important information is easily viewable and understandable, even on the lowest-resolution settings. Not everyone has fast enough Internet to watch videos in HD, so it's very important to make your content accessible to everybody.

3. **Your aim is to sell your products, so make sure you include a clear call to action.** After watching your video, viewers should want to order your products and services right away.

4. **Make sure your video is exciting or humorous or both, to keep the viewer's attention.**

5. **Be aware that people won't watch a one-hour video on YouTube.** Web and video experts, like those at Veeroll.com, say you have only ten seconds to entice the viewer. If you miss this opportunity, your visitor will probably click away and never return. Always keep it short, and get to the point early on in the video. Try to keep your total video length to two or three minutes.

6. **Make sure the lighting of your video is ideal and your camera isn't shaking.** There are great tools to achieve top-quality video production at very little cost. Simply Google "lighting and camera kits" and you can find something that will even make shooting with your iPhone appear profesionally done.

7. **It's very important that the speech in your video is clear so your audience doesn't have to make an effort to understand what you're saying.** Background music is great, but it shouldn't be so loud it drowns out the the narration.

8. **Prepare your movie editing software.** Almost every computer comes with some kind of movie editing software (e.g., Windows Movie Maker, Apple iMovie). If you don't have one, there are plenty of free programs online. Familiarize yourself with the basic features before starting to edit. Camtasia is an excellent program that allows for screencapture and video editing, though it only offers a free trial.

   Post your video on your website, as well as any other social media sites. A video is a big investment for your business, so you need to do everything you can to blast it out there. YouTube advertisements are very effective in increasing the views and click-throughs of your video. Most video-sharing platforms allow you to upload different video formats, though most limit file size. YouTube, for example, allows 100 MB per video.

· 6 ·

Online Advertising and PPC

· · · · · · · · ·

WELCOME TO THE new frontier in advertising online. You may not be selling your product or business here yet, but you should be. According to a recent survey, 93 percent of online experiences start with a search engine (Source: Search Engine Journal). Your competitors are probably online already (more on that in a minute), so you need to be as well, or your business will suffer.

This chapter will help you get started. It includes some basic strategies for creating banner ads and other kinds of online commercials, plus a short introduction to pay-per-click (PPC) and Google AdWords to extend your marketing campaign beyond SEO. While SEO produces organic search results, pay-per-click results refer to the advertisements on the top and the side of Google search results and on Facebook pages.

Creating the Perfect Online Banner Ad

BANNER ADS PICK up where newspapers and magazines left off. Imagine that pay-per-click (PPC) word ads are like the classified section of a newspaper, and the banner ads are all the fancy display ads in the rest of the paper. Traditionally, classified ads are for people who are looking for something they need. On the other hand, display ads are for building brand awareness and pushing your message to the consumer.

The great thing about online banner ads compared to print display ads is the interactivity you can create with it. You can use animations to draw attention and give your ad some energy, making it more compelling than it would be in print.

There is, of course, a drawback. The jury is still out on how successful banner ads are. Are people really clicking on your ads? Are they even paying attention? Acquiring an ad impression (i.e., how many eyeballs actually see your ad) is one of the basic philosophies in advertising. The more impressions you get, the more likely you are to build your brand and get people buying your product or service. The great thing with online banner ads is the data that you can get before and after you place the ad. The more data you have in advertising, the more precise you can be with how you spend your money.

8 Key Elements of a Great Banner Ad

THESE EIGHT ELEMENTS come courtesy of advertising strategist Todd Garland, who designed and outlined the eight "key elements" in a banner ad.

1. **Interactivity:** Make your ad more than just a static image. Adding sound and animation can help it stand out against the live elements of the web page and improve your brand awareness by as much as 64 percent.

2. **Good use of space:** Cluttering your ad with too much information will cause viewers to potentially ignore your ad. Use space effectively and let your ad stretch! Don't try to fit all of your content into one ad. If you have too much information, make multiple banner ads.

3. **Compelling imagery:** Pictures work harder than words. Use images that express the philosophy of your business. Also, avoid photos that look like they were bought from Getty Images. Unique images draw in readers!

4. **Creative message:** Think of fun, interesting ways to convey your point. Readers will ignore mundane text, so make it tantalizing.

5. **Call to action:** Make your ad interactive by providing a way for readers to purchase your product easily. Avoid clichéd links, like "click here." Elicit curiosity and excitement from the reader.

6. **Brand incorporation:** Employ the same colors, fonts, and logos that you use for your logo and other marketing campaigns. If your ad doesn't match the brand identity of your business, you may confuse the reader.

7. **Strong text:** If space is limited, you should use big, strong words to attract attention. Avoid soft or passive words. Write in the present tense.

8. **Appropriate humor:** Humor injects personality into your ad, while also making it more memorable.

4 Things Not to Do In Your Banner Ad

1. **Don't lose the message.** Don't let the words kill the visual appeal of your ad—you'll bore your audience.

2. **Don't make false promises.** While this tactic will generate a higher click-through rate, it'll yield few sales, if any, and will leave your audience feeling cheated.

3. **Don't overuse strong language.** While you should use strong language, let it supplement graphics and enticements. Simply saying "BUY NOW" won't generate new sales.

4. **Don't use too many colors.** Bright colors may attract an initial glance but they're also likely to scare your audience away. Don't turn your banner into a neon rainbow!

What Is Pay-Per-Click Advertising on Search Engines?

PAY-PER-CLICK (PPC) IS named after the pricing structure used by some online channels to charge advertisers. When a user clicks on an ad, the advertiser is then charged. In most cases, the online channel will work on a price-bidding structure, with the advertiser specifying the maximum they want to spend.

The pay-per-click model is one used for advertising on search engines such as Google, Yahoo, and Bing. It works for both parties because the search engines are guaranteed income, while advertisers have better online visibility with low, capped costs.

3 Benefits of Pay-Per-Click Advertising

1. **Fast results:** While search engine optimization (SEO) takes time to build, PPC enables advertisers to compete within their market immediately based on the budget they're willing to spend.
2. **Decide your own budget:** You control your budget and can spend as little or as much as you want. There may be a particular time of year when your business benefits from a higher advertising budget. If so, you can adjust your budget accordingly.
3. **Track your results:** One of the great features of PPC on search engines is you can track how well it's working. The search engines all have tools that can be set up so the advertiser can see what keywords and ads are driving traffic to their website. You can even see which ones are generating the most leads or sales.

Is PPC For Me?

NEXT I WLLL show you how pay-per-click advertising works. After you've read this section, you'll need to decide if it's something you want to pursue yourself, or outsource. It can take time to learn the system, then set it up and put it in place, so you may find it more effective to outsource to another company.

The only way to decide is to dip your toes into the water and see how you fare. Google usually offers new customers $100 credit to test out the service, so use it to get a good handle on PPC before you spend any money.

Is the Competition Using It?

IMAGINE FRED WANTS to test out PPC to see if it's the right online advertising tool for his bakery business. How should he go about it?

A great starting point would be to set up a Google AdWords account. Bing or Yahoo work too, but for this example we will use Google. Over 80 percent of Internet users do their searching with Google. With their ongoing promotion of $100 free advertising for new users, it's enough for Fred to dabble online for a few days and decide if this is the best route for his business.

But first, Fred should check if his competitors are using PPC. If he types some relevant keywords, such as "cakes" and "cupcakes," into Google to see if his competitors' company name appears in the sponsored ads, and they do, chances are these keywords indicate a strong return on investment for his competitors, and Fred should consider competing with those words.

On the other hand, if Fred's search doesn't present any bakeries in the sponsored ads section, Google AdWords may not be worth pursuing. Either there's a gap in the market or his competitors have tried it and didn't see a solid return on investment.

Before you set up a Google AdWords account, you want to be clear of your goals. Are you looking to sell a product online, gain a lead, or get a user to subscribe?

Setting up Your PPC Campaign

IN THIS SECTION, I'll walk you through how to set up your own PPC campaign. PPC, and ensuring that you are found by paying for it, is key to your business's success online. But don't worry—it's easier than you might think.

CHOOSING YOUR AD GROUPS

FRED'S DECIDED THAT he needs to use Google AdWords to promote his cupcake range. So, first, he creates a new campaign called "Cupcake." Within his new campaign, he then needs to create ad groups (i.e., the different ad categories in his campaign). In this example, Fred sets up five ad groups to represent the five types of cupcakes he sells:
- Cupcakes
- Birthday cupcakes
- Children's cupcakes
- Custom cupcakes
- Wedding cupcakes

CHOOSING YOUR KEYWORDS

NOW THAT FRED has outlined his target groups, the next step is to create keyword lists for each category. He can do this by performing a keyword analysis. The "birthday cupcake" ad group will have keywords focused just on this subject (e.g., birthday cakes, cupcakes for birthdays, and birthday cupcakes). See the SEO section on how to conduct a keyword analysis.

CREATING YOUR ADS: 7 GUIDELINES FOR EFFECTIVE GOOGLE ADWORDS COPY

NOW IT'S TIME for Fred to write some great, eye-catching copy. He should follow these seven guidelines:

1. **Don't write generic ad copy for all of the ad groups.** Make sure the copy is tailored to each ad group and its set of keywords.

For example, if a user searches for "birthday cupcakes," make sure they see an ad relevant to birthdays and cupcakes.

2. **Make sure your message is clear and concise.** There's very little space to get your message across, so make sure it summarizes your unique selling point. What makes your brand, products, or services better than those of your closest rivals?

3. **Be sure to include a call to action.** Why should a potential customer click on your ad? Is it to get a quote? To schedule an appointment? Advertisers need to give customers a reason to care—and click.

4. **The display** URL **will also show up on the ad.** This doesn't have to be exactly the same as the click-through URL. However, it should include the basic elements of the address to be consistent.

5. **Never use slang words or "text" speak.** Always use proper spelling and punctuation.

6. **Never make any false claims.**

7. **Always test different ads against each other.** Find out which ad is getting the better response rates. That is the only way you'll improve your Google AdWords campaign. Within each ad group, make sure you always have two to three ads running in rotation. The elements of the ads you'll want to test are
   - the titles;
   - the calls to action; and
   - your unique selling points.

Good Ads versus Bad Ads

TESTING IS A great way to improve what you already have. However, never test more than one variable at a time. This will help you narrow your marketing focus to the most likely audience willing to spend the most money with you. Once you've tested many different variables one by one, you should have an optimum selection of ad copy that works hard to bring you new business.

Cupcakes in Vancouver
www.FredsBakery.com/cupcakes ▾
We make the best cupcakes in town.
Order online in one click.

The good ad

Fred's Bakery Cakes
www.FredsBakery.com ▾
We have delicious cakes!
Find out more today!

The bad ad

Both of these ads are designed to show up when the term "Cupcakes in Vancouver" is searched. Here's why the good ad works better.

The title of the good ad includes the keywords the user searched. This relevancy and consistency will immediately draw the user's eye. The title of the bad ad is too generic and isn't directly relevant to the user's search. They don't know nor care who Fred is. They just want some cakes.

The second line of the good ad works well because Fred's Bakery has won awards in Vancouver, which is their unique selling point. The bad ad also sells them as a leading bakery, but the use of slang wouldn't impress users.

The good ad has a strong call to action (i.e., "Order Online"), while the bad ad is too vague (i.e., "Find out More Today"). Be sure to tell the user what they need to do.

Finally, the display URL in the good ad is consistent with the title and keywords, while the bad ad just shows the generic website address.

What's Quality Score?

QUALITY SCORE IS an important part of PPC if you want to appear higher in the search rankings while paying less than your competitors.

Google AdWords decides how relevant your business is to a user's search by examining your keyword lists, the ad copy these are related to, and the landing page the copy clicks through to. Google also looks at your historical data, such as response rates.

Make sure the keywords in your list can be found consistently within your ad copy and within the text on your landing page. If your historical data also shows high response rates from your keywords over the last year, chances are Google will give you a high-quality score.

Your quality score affects the price you pay per bid on your keywords, as well as your ranking position. If your score is higher than your competitors', you'll pay less for a higher ranking compared to them.

The score is out of ten, with one being the lowest and ten the highest, and you can view your score on the keyword tab of the AdWords page. Remember, quality scores take time to build. Be patient, comply with the rules, and you'll see the improvements soon enough.

Landing Pages

A LANDING PAGE is the one-page website a potential customer sees after clicking on an advertisement. As such, it needs to have attention-grabbing content. The purpose of the landing page is to draw the consumer straight in and make sure they keep reading. It should be clear, specific, and easy to navigate and almost always has an opt-in feature that enables people to make a purchase.

Be Sure to Create Landing Pages for Your Campaign

CREATING LANDING PAGES for a PPC campaign can make the difference between success and failure. For many businesses, it's not enough to have all online advertisements linking to the home page of their website. This is especially true of PPC campaigns. People expect something when they click an ad. If they're sent to a generic welcome page, you can bet they'll turn around and leave the site.

Let's use Fred's Bakery as our example again. Fred has a great home page on his website. He has large images of his creations, including cakes, donuts, pastries, and bread. To top it off, he has a concise paragraph of text explaining what his business is.

When Fred put his Google AdWords campaign live, he pointed all of his ads to the home page. But this had two negative effects on his response.

Firstly, when a potential customer clicked on an ad about cupcakes, they landed on his home page, which describes this type of confection as just one of his many baking services. To find the information they were looking for—namely cupcakes—they had to browse his website to find the cupcake page. You might think this isn't a big deal, but Internet users are notoriously impatient, and want the answer immediately. They don't want to click around a website to find it. If you make it hard for them, they'll just click away—probably to your competitor next door.

The second problem is the home page text lowered Fred's quality score. Although his home page mentions cupcakes, it's just a small portion of his content. His competitors have cupcake-only landing pages, so Google awards them higher scores.

Fred realizes he needs to create some landing pages for his Google AdWords campaign, one for each ad group he had set up. For the cupcakes ad group, he created a landing page using the URL FredsBakery.com/Cup-Cakes. The page featured the following information:

- Fred's cupcake services;
- examples of previous projects;
- an order form (the clear call to action); and
- contact information for the bakery.

Fred and his team set up a really effective landing page. Google was happy with its relevancy, and Fred saw his quality score improve. More people ordered cupcakes because they were finding all the information they needed on the one page, and they didn't have to click anywhere else.

7 Must-Have Features for Your Landing Page

1. **A great headline:** This should be attention-grabbing, short, and direct. What do you want people to do? Why should they do it?
2. **A concise, clear offer:** Put this in large lettering directly under the headline.
3. **A call to action:** Your landing page should tell people to purchase your product *now*. Direct them as they carry out their order. Using images and videos to support your call-to-action can be very effective.
4. **A time-sensitive offer for those who opt in now:** Bonuses, discounts, and other promotions will entice people to make a purchase immediately.

5. **A subscription link or page that's very noticeable:** Be sure people who want to make a purchase can find the right link.
6. **An outline of the security features for credit cards:** Reassure people that their information is secure and the purchase will go through without any hiccups.
7. **A thank-you page or after-purchase message:** People look for the "thank-you" to confirm that their order has gone through. Sending a thank-you email with follow-up offers may even generate further sales.

3 Key Features of Your Bonus Product

CONSIDER OFFERING A bonus product before or after the front-end purchase. Whether it's offered in a thank-you email or advertised on the landing page, the bonus product should have the following features, to increase the conversion rate:

1. **It should complement the initial product.** Ideally, your bonus product will augment the features of the primary purchase, making it a better product for the customer.
2. **It should be reinforced by your business as much as the initial product.** The bonus product copy or reviews, if available, should be described glowingly. You don't want the bonus product to look like an unnecessary add-on, but as an amazing product on its own.
3. **It should be time-sensitive, requiring immediate action.**

Setting Your Budget

A STARTING POINT in setting your budget is to find out how much your keywords will cost when people click on them. AdWords has a free tool that estimates traffic from your keywords and the average cost per click. Remember, your industry affects your cost per click. If you're in an extremely competitive niche, your cost per click will he higher. For this reason, it would be wise to do a traffic estimation report to help set your budget.

You should also consider how many people you want to drive to your website. Fred's Bakery estimated that only 10 percent of customers who visit their website end up calling or ordering online. Fred wants to make five sales from his website each day, so he needs fifty visitors a day to reach his target. He checked Google's traffic estimator and saw that he would have to pay $1.50 per click on average for his keywords. Therefore, his daily budget would be set to at least $75 per day.

The best way for you to set your budget is to find out what your goal is and work back from there, just like Fred.

Optimizing Your PPC Campaign

SO HOW CAN you tell how successful your PPC campaign is? How can you get feedback to improve the results?

Google provides you with a tracking code that allows you to see not only the number of orders that Google AdWords produces, but also the exact ad users viewed and the keywords that were searched. This information is invaluable in determining what is and isn't working for your campaign, going forward, which saves your business time and money too.

Once you have your tracking code in place, optimizing your campaign is much easier. In an ideal world, you would be doing this on a weekly basis. At this stage, what's important is your customers can find you online, whether that's through effective SEO or PPC on the search engines.

Once this is all in place and working for your business, you can then look into other PPC options. Google is just one example, but they also have a display network. This allows advertisers to use text ads, image ads, and video ads on websites. Google even has a service for ads on mobile websites. All of these models can be bought on a PPC basis, within the same parameters as Google AdWords. Therefore, an advertiser can control all of their online marketing from the same dashboard, reaching out to a wider audience at a potentially cost-effective price.

Online advertisements can no longer be ignored by retailers and businesses if they want to survive. People decide what they want to buy and who they want to buy it from through the Internet and search engines. It's your responsibility to get your name out there on Google and other search engines before your business gets buried by the competition.

Mobile Advertising and Marketing

MOBILE ADVERTISING AND marketing are relatively new tactics for reaching consumers. But they'll only get bigger. Recent reports state 91 percent of US citizens have a cell phone, and each user checks their phone around 150 times per day. The explosion of short message service (SMS) texts is fueling this growth.

4 Tools and Resources for Doing Your Own PPC

If you decide to move forward and become a PPC expert, the tools and resources listed below will help you research and manage your campaigns.

1. **WordStream.com:** WordStream is a great tool to help you optimize your PPC. It gives keyword recommendations—as well as negative keyword suggestions—and it also has a tool that analyzes where you need to improve your campaign.
2. **AdWords Editor:** This is a Google tool that's a bit more user-friendly than their web page version.
3. **Google Traffic Estimator:** This helps to estimate keyword traffic.
4. **Google Keyword Tool:** This helps to build your keyword lists.

SMS Marketing

SMS MARKETING IS a relatively inexpensive way to reach a large population of consumers. Sending out a thousand texts a month only costs about $10. Even cell phone users with no mobile Internet access receive SMS texts, so these messages are widely distributed. And the results are immediate: the average text is opened four minutes after it's sent.

MMS Marketing

MULTIMEDIA MESSAGING SERVICES (MMS) marketing campaigns have increased in popularity as smartphones have become the de facto mobile phone. MMS enable audio, video, and visual graphics to be sent via text messaging. Although pricier, MMS marketing campaigns are visually more attractive and typically yield better response rates than SMS campaigns.

Proximity Marketing

PROXIMITY MARKETING—OR BLUETOOTH marketing—has yet to make a serious mark in North America, but the idea is full of potential. People in an extremely localized area whose phones are Bluetooth-enabled will receive an alert asking them if they'll accept a text message. The great thing about proximity marketing is that you can target people who are in highly specific geographic areas. Targeting can be narrowed even further. For example, if you're selling a service to tourists, your message

---

2 Great Online Resources for SEO Industry News and Best Practices

1. searchenginejournal.com
2. searchengineland.com

can be limited to people in a specific area whose device is registered from outside of the city.

Proximity marketing can also be limited to specific times and dates, such as a three-hour period when an event is taking place.

Mobile Apps

MOBILE APPS ARE secure, fast, and created specifically for mobile devices, meaning they're easy to navigate. Apps can be quite expensive to produce, however, so only consider making one if you think it'll provide substantial value for your current customers or potential customers.

If you provide a service or a product that customers regularly use (e.g., local flights, gym classes), an app that provides updates on schedules, hours, or new products could enhance your business. If your business provides instructional expertise, like diet assistance, inserting some lessons on an app could boost business (e.g., "3 Healthy Menus to Get You Through the Day").

SECTION 3

Traditional Advertising and Public Relations

SO NOW YOU'RE up to speed with all the hot stuff online, but to take your business to the next level, you have go back in time to move forward. Let's consider some old-school methods that can still create a big buzz for you business.

As an agency owner, I am asked by clients to ignore traditional media more and more. First, they started moving away from advertising, but now they're also starting to move away from PR. I think it's premature to ignore traditional media channels to get your message out, whether they're paid channels or not. The Buzz Formula still works. Remember, the intention here is to focus your communications campaign and maximize every penny spent. If you're launching—or even re-launching—your brand, you want to be in front of as many consumers as possible within the budget you've set aside.

In recent years, there have been some major examples of this. In Canada, a national dairy company recently launched its new yogurt product line. Yogurt is a highly competitive product, and grabbing a share of the market is a risky and often expensive venture. However, for one month this yogurt brand was everywhere: advertisements on billboards, in print, on TV and radio, and online. They also got a major PR push. It was a massive, national, multi-million-dollar campaign.

Their intention for the campaign was to make consumers feel—after about two months of inundating them with advertisements—that this yogurt brand had been around forever. They wanted the product line branded into people's minds so that trust was achieved. It worked. And now that brand is one of the top sellers in the grocery store aisle. What's interesting is that campaign followed the same basic structure of the Buzz Formula, except on a *massive* scale. So whether it's $5,000 or $5 million, the principles are the same.

· 7 ·

Media Buying and Promotions

· · · · · · · · ·

NOW, AS A small business owner, deciding to do your own advertising can be daunting, but this book is meant to empower you.

First off, it's important to give you a few key definitions to provide you with the confidence you need to get going on your own. Many newcomers confuse advertising with media buying. The creative work of actually conceiving and designing advertisements—the stuff Don Draper does on *Mad Men*—is traditionally called advertising. The procurement of media real estate at optimal placement and price point is media buying, a subset of advertising management. The big challenge in media buying lies in negotiating the best price and placement for your ad, whether it's in print, radio, TV, or outdoor billboards.

Too many businesses buy media exposure without knowing proper rates or which media to invest in. It's no wonder they spend large amounts of money on advertising without seeing significant results. Media buying is all about knowing what outlet is right for your business and how much the advertising there will cost.

The purpose of advertising is to encourage or persuade an audience to take a specific action. Advertising aims to control and direct a consumer's behavior.

Every ad aims to deliver the desired call to action in a way the audience will find engaging, entertaining, and easy to understand. Your ad doesn't need to tell the audience explicitly what to do. Actions and images can often speak louder than words. Persuasion is an act of gentle pulling, not vigorous pushing. Examples of calls to action can be as simple as "Buy now," "Call 555-5555 to learn more," or "Visit out website for more information." On the more creative side, Subway's recognized call to action is "Think fresh, eat fresh."

Remember, not every call to action needs to make a sale. They're also an important part of the information-gathering process.

The Marketing Funnel

FOR OVER A century, the marketing funnel has been the de facto method for attracting consumers. While social media has made marketing more of a conversation between the customer and business or brand, the marketing funnel is still a useful framework for your advertising campaigns. It can be broken down into the acronym AIDA: attention, interest, desire, and action. AIDA is a useful way to look at any new advertising campaign because it highlights the process that goes into creating new sales.

A – Attention: Attract the customer's attention. E.g., an attention-grabbing headline

I – Interest: Generate interest by demonstrating the qualities of the product and why the customer would want to purchase it.

D – Desire: Create a need for the product. Entice the consumers through promises and product results.

A – Action: Create a call to action that compels the consumer to make a purchase.

Media Buying

WHEN YOU'RE LOOKING at the perfect ad price and medium to increase the reach of your ad, you're buying media. Since every ad needs to be placed somewhere, media buying is an important part of your marketing campaign.

Purchasing media real estate is at least as complex as buying physical real estate. That new home has to fit your needs and interests. You have to consider its size, location, and price.

Perhaps most importantly, you need to think about the target audience, an aspect you can safely ignore when buying a house.

The starting point here is thorough research. You need to identify your target audience, analyze its demographic, geographic, and psychographic composition, and decide what media type you want to use. While your budget is an important factor, careful planning is essential in determining when and where to air, print, or post your ad.

Let's look at an example. Say you're trying to promote a fashion product for teenage girls. Your decision on where to place the ad is as important as the ad itself. Put it in the news section of a Sunday paper and you won't reach as much of your target audience as you would if you aired it as a commercial during *The Bachelor*. On the other hand, your budget may be too tight for TV. This is why you need to evaluate carefully what media placement is best suited for your campaign in order to secure the best possible return on investment (ROI).

6 Factors to Consider When Buying Media

1. What's your target **demographic** compared with that of the media outlet? What's their age? Price range? Sex? Race? Nationality? Income level? Do they have children? The demographics of your business and the media outlet should be similar.
2. What are the **psychographic** factors of your consumers compared with those of the media outlet? What are their interests? Hobbies? Passions? Are they readers? Do they watch TV?
3. What's the **geographic** area of your consumer base? Are your readers, listeners, or viewers from the same region as the audience of the media outlet? This is very important because you could have the most appealing commercial in the world, but it wouldn't make a difference because the consumers live too far away from the actual store.
4. What **time** of the day does your audience tune in to the program?

5. Can you afford the **prices** the media outlet is asking for? Are they priced competitively, or can you find better value elsewhere?

6. Is there any **room for negotiation** on the prices? Are there discounts available if you commit to a certain number of media buys?

Which Media Outlet Should You Buy From?

CHOOSING WHICH MEDIA outlet to work with can be difficult. Start with the Buzz Formula. Don't settle for the first outlet you reach a deal with. Remember, the media *needs* your advertising dollars. Media relations means catering to the editorial department, but, when dealing with the advertising department, the roles are reversed. You just need to make sure you're getting the best value for your dollar.

3 Steps in Choosing the Right Media Buy

1. **Identify and research your target market.** Market research will give you insight into your market's demographics. You want to know whether your customers read papers and magazines, listen to the radio, or watch TV. Study their behavior and what medium they're most likely to use.

2. **Set your own objectives.** Are you looking to increase sales and subscriptions? Do you want to increase publicity or your reputation? Certain media outlets may not increase sales but are viewed as extremely trustworthy. Do you want to reach a broad audience or a well-defined audience? Answering questions like these will help you decide what your media-buying strategy should be going forward.

3. **Identify your budget.** Advertising on TV and in national newspapers and popular magazines costs more than advertising with regional newspapers and radio shows. You need to be realistic about your budget and be careful not to put all your eggs into one basket.

Detailed Media Outlet Analysis

AT CURVE WE recommend answers to these questions every time you negotiate a media buy. Use this as a checklist to make sure you have all the information you need to make a fully informed decision.

- How much of your target audience does this media outlet reach?
- Does the media outlet meet your desired schedule, and can it guarantee placement dates and where the ad will land on the page or air, on the TV or radio station?
- What are the costs?
  - Negotiated rate
  - Rate card rate
  - Savings per advertisement
  - Overall savings
  - Total costs
- Is the media outlet offering bonus placements for buying with them?
- Is the media outlet offering any other added value to the placement? Could they offer free e-blasts or an email directory?
- Why this media outlet? What's the reasoning behind buying media space with this outlet versus another one?

Media Sponsorship

MEDIA SPONSORSHIPS AND promotions are two additional types of advertising that are helpful if you're hosting an event or a launch. To get a media sponsor, you generally negotiate when you're placing your advertising. If you're holding an event or there is some added benefit for the media outlet in having their name associated with your venture, that value can be added as a bonus to how much money you are spending with a media outlet. These value-added promotions will round out your advertising campaign, and, if you're making a significant media ad buy, you should expect to get some extra promotion to support it.

The Most Common Media Promotions in Radio, TV, and Newspapers

RADIO AND TV

- Two-for-one—or one-for-one—ad buys are often extended to non-profit event organizers.
- Pre-produced promotional spots are very valuable and usually center on on-air promotions for listeners of the station, like ticket giveaways or winning a special night out. These promotions often involve retailers. Listeners have to visit a store to pick up an entry form.
- Traffic or news sponsorships or bonuses are ten- to five-second acknowledgments that are centered on the news, sports, or traffic reports; for example, "Traffic today brought to you by Curve Communications," or something like that.
- Community cruiser mentions are on-air from radio hosts on location. You hear these when a new store opens or is having a big sale and they want people to come down and check it out.
- Live-liners are live, on-air announcements made by the DJ throughout the broadcast.

NEWSPAPER

- **Promotional ads with a contest element.** These are effective if you are trying to collect information about your customers or build your lists. The newspaper will often control the contest but sometimes will give you all the details of who entered once the contest is over.

- **Donated space in the newspaper.** This is most effective for non-profits, but sometimes your business may have a cause it wants to promote or support, and donated, sometimes called remnant space, can be very valuable and useful.
- **Other promotional possibilities include website and mobile ads, newspaper promotional material giveaways, and access to email lists.** Each of these may be offered up as incentives to have your business advertise in a particular newspaper.

· 8 ·

Creating Advertisements

· · · · · · · · ·

WE PASS BY billboards in our cars. We stare at posters at transit shelters. We hear commercials on the radio. We get interrupted by pop-ups on our free apps. Advertising is *everywhere*. How do you stand above the rest?

Great creative is a mixture of many elements, but what it comes down to is this: focusing on simple techniques and messaging will increase the engagement level of your ad and its effectiveness. Here's an example of a basic ad script that tells the customer everything they need to know.

> Person 1: Did you hear about that great sale?
> Person 2: No! Where is this great sale?
> Person 1: It's at Company X at Company X's address this Saturday!
> Person 2: Wow. What kind of deals are there?
> Person 1: They'll have Products A, B, *and* C on sale! Major discounts!
> Person 2: I guess we know where we're going this Saturday!
> Together: To Company X at Company X's address this Saturday, between ten and two!

The previous ad hits all the main points: company name, company address, and the fact that they're having a big sale with products A, B, and C discounted. Now you can zest things up with art, sound, characters, and so on. But remember that you must always keep in mind the key points you are trying to convey.

A radio station once advertised a *you-pick-they-grill* type restaurant with a "Vegetable Medley," featuring singing veggies. Campy? Sure. Fun? Absolutely. Another radio station once advertised a car dealership with an on-going soap opera, featuring the usual, dramatic trials and tribulations—evil twins, love affairs, etc.—set in a car dealership. Recently, Dodge used Ron Burgundy, the movie character made famous by actor Will Ferrell, to extol not the virtues of the Durango itself but, specifically, the glove compartment.

All these ads resulted in higher sales because they made people pay attention. Our attention is constantly distracted by a million different sources, so you need to make your message really stand out, be it on TV, radio, or a poster, while at the same time remembering that you also need to inform the audience.

Creating the Perfect Print Ad

THE CREATIVE ASPECT of advertising is definitely exciting, and I'm sure you're excited to jump right in. However, before you start creating your great newspaper or magazine ad, you need to make sure it'll be a success. The quality of your ad is the single most important determinant of advertising effectiveness. Ask yourself, does your ad have these qualities?

- **Is your ad appealing?** Every ad needs to include a call to action. This is particularly important for print ads. Always include your company's phone number, website, or address. People read newspapers to get news, so why not make your ad newsworthy? And while the headline is important, remember that an image is worth a thousand words.

- **Is your ad attention-getting?** For newspapers in particular, color is essential in capturing the attention of a reader. Adding even a single color to your advertisement can dramatically increase the number of people who read your ad.

  If your budget is tight, many newspapers will offer free design. However, this doesn't necessarily guarantee it'll be a great ad—it all depends on their design team. I recommend either working closely with their staff or hiring a professional copywriter and designer.

- **Does it communicate the main message?** You have very little time to get your message across, once the reader's eyes land on your ad. An image and a headline are the most important carriers of your message. They need to state clearly what it is that you're offering. Be consistent in your message. Make sure the reader becomes familiar with your main message so they'll recognize it among other ads.

- **Is it believable?** Your print advertising campaign won't succeed overnight—success stems from trustworthiness and familiarity. The more you advertise and establish your company as a trustworthy one, the more believable you'll appear to your audience.

- **Is it persuasive?** Your ad should tell a story from a particular point of view. Make it convincing! The whole point of your ad is to leave an impression on the viewer. Whatever product or service you're advertising, you need to give them just enough information to persuade the viewer to go and look your company up.

Where to Put Your Newspaper Ad

THE MOST COMMON newspaper formats are tabloid, Berliner, and broadsheet. The ideal positioning of a print ad depends on the format.

Broadsheet format is traditionally associated with a more educated readership, though some claim it's now obsolete, since it's unsuitable for reading in public transit, where a lot of newspapers are read.

Berliner format is slightly taller and wider than tabloid, but narrower and shorter than broadsheet. It's only used to describe the dimensions of the paper, not the type of content within it.

Tabloid format has traditionally been associated with sensational reporting, but, though there are still a lot of splashy, scandal-focused papers, it's becoming increasingly common for serious papers as well, especially the free commuter dailies launching in markets around the world.

5 Tips for Placing Your Newspaper Ad

1. **Place your ad as far forward in the paper as possible, preferably in the news section.**
2. **If the newspaper has a fold, place your ad above it.** A reader's attention wanes dramatically as they move down a page.
3. **If the newspaper is divided into thematic sections, choose the one most likely to attract your target customer group.** If your business is in the business of selling kitchen appliances, the lifestyle, cooking, or health sections will yield more results than sports or automotive.
4. **Look at the left-hand page and draw an imaginary diagonal line from the upper left corner to the lower right.** Do the same on the right-hand page, this time drawing the line from right to left. Newspapers typically run news and editorials above the fold and place ads in the triangle below it, but it's possible to nab the tiny gap just above the fold on the left or right before

your ad gets lost among all the others. This is the prime advertising spot. Obviously ads here can't be big, but the position more than makes up for this.

5. **To dominate a page in the newspaper, you don't have to buy a full-page ad.** A half- to three-quarter-page ad with great design is proven to have the same effect as a full-page ad at a much lower cost.

Where to Put Your Magazine Ad

IT'S GENERALLY HELD that the most cost-effective magazine advertising is found in the following places (in order of cost effectiveness):

- back of the magazine;
- inside page one;
- inside the front cover; and
- inside the back cover.

In these locations, your ad will reach both the people who purchased the magazine and any casual browsers who might flip through it at the newsstand or supermarket.

Creating the Perfect Radio Ad

DESPITE THE ONSLAUGHT of TV, computers, the Internet, and social media, radio is still holding its own as an important advertising platform. Not only is it affordable—especially compared to TV—but it can also reach both mass audiences and niche target groups, depending on the character of the radio station.

Target Your Radio Audience

UNDERSTANDING YOUR TARGET audience is key to every successful marketing strategy, and radio is no exception. Radio stations often focus on specific segments of the population. Country music channels, for instance, tend to target older listeners, while contemporary dance hit stations are aimed at teenagers.

So how should you decide which radio stations best suit your marketing goals? Start by spending some time listening to your local radio stations, and note what music they play, who calls in to which broadcasts, what the general tone of the emcees are, etc. Then write down a short target audience profile that includes information such as age, gender, income, and any other factors that are relevant to your campaign.

Next, call the sales representatives of the radio stations you're considering and share this information with them. Advertising and target audiences are their bread and butter, and they'll help you pinpoint the best airtime for your ad. You need to do your own research to make the most out of your radio ad buy.

Frequency and Appeal of Radio Ads

LIKE ALL ADS, radio commercials need to be aired over and over again before they capture the listener's attention. Scheduling your ad to air once a month won't do. You'll have to buy ads with enough frequency to make sure your campaign reaches your target audience many times over.

Although radio is still predominantly listened to in cars, many listeners are now tuning in online. These listeners—and potential customers—are just a click away from your website, so your ad needs to appeal directly to them.

Your message needs to be compelling and easy to grasp. In other words, it needs to have a wow factor. People often listen to radio subconsciously, while they're busy driving or doing the dishes, so design your ad to make them sit up and give you their full attention.

Designing Your Radio Ad

THE BEAUTY OF radio is its lack of visuals. You're working with the theatre of the mind, and there are virtually no boundaries to your creativity. Radio ads engage listeners in a six- to thirty-second story, which is all the time you have to get your message across.

So how do you go about writing a radio ad? Start with the central idea of your campaign. Whether this is the effectiveness of your service or the launch of a new product, your central idea needs to be simple and easy to understand.

Build a written script around the idea, making sure that your company or product name and your website or phone number are mentioned at least three times. Refrain from complicated sentences, and don't overwhelm the listener with numbers or random facts. The pacing of your script should also match the style of the radio stations your ad will air on. Once you have a working script, you need to choose a suitable voiceover. Not every voice works on radio, so it's often worth conducting a short casting.

Finally, consider adding sound elements to enhance your message. Background music and sound effects are the most common techniques. Commissioning a catchy jingle that's easy to remember and that can accompany several of your company's ads is another good way of attracting listeners' attention. Since the entire advertisement experience is auditory, having a catchy tune is paramount to the success of the ad.

Producing a Radio Ad

RADIO ADS ARE relatively easy to produce, at least compared to TV or outdoor sign campaigns. All you need is appropriate software and a microphone. You can download recording and audio editing software online, and free tools such as Audacity or GarageBand are perfectly adequate.

If you want more high-quality recording software, there are a few paid programs you can download that have more functionality, like Camtasia, Premiere, and Vegas. There are also various sound effects databases online, where you can find sound elements to complete your ad. If you decide to use background music that's not of your own creation, you're obliged to comply with existing copyright legislation. Be careful here: being sued for infringing on copyright laws can significantly damage your company's image. Since the sound quality of your ad is important, you may wish to consult an audio engineer to make sure everything sounds the best it can. It's tempting to cut costs and use what you have available, but be warned, your computer's built-in microphone isn't good enough for recording a successful radio ad.

For a small fee—or sometimes included as part of your radio advertising package—the station will write, record, and produce your commercial for you. In-house production quality can vary from station to station, so stay engaged, and don't be afraid to have them reproduce the piece until you're satisfied.

The Radio Broadcast Day

RADIO BROADCAST HOURS are typically divided into different segments based on the audience. The standard segments are as follows:

Morning drive time: 6:00 a.m. to 10:00 a.m.

Daytime: 10:00 a.m. to 3:00 p.m.

Afternoon drive time: 3:00 p.m. to 7:00 p.m.

Evening: 7:00 p.m. to 12:00 a.m.

Late night: 12:00 a.m. to 6:00 a.m.

Creating the Perfect TV Ad

TV ADVERTISING MAY seem like the realm of billion-dollar corporations. This is understandable. TV commercials pay massive production costs even before going to air, and all that hard work is only seen in thirty-second segments. It also doesn't help that your ad will be played in between segments from Coca-Cola, Adidas, Nike, or Gucci.

Don't be discouraged! It's possible to make money from TV advertising. This section will outline the best way for you to maximize your sales through TV commercials without breaking the bank.

How to Make a Successful "Immediate Response" Commercial

MOST TV ADS are image or brand advertising. These types of ads are selling an emotion about a company or a product. They tend to be quite artistic and expensive, and take a long time to yield financial results. This is because image advertisements don't have a call to action selling a specific product. Instead, they work by constantly bombarding the consumer with an idea or emotion until she's convinced that the brand will improve her life.

Unless you're Coca-Cola, this type of advertising is probably financially impossible for your business. Instead, you'll need to learn how to make a successful "immediate response" commercial. These commercials are all about getting down to business. The consumer is told about the product, where they can get it, why they need it, and why they should get it right now. Immediate response TV ads create an effective call to action that will increase sales right away. If you need fast results and don't have a ton of money in your advertising budget, immediate response ads are the ones for you.

5 Tips for Planning Your TV Ad

1. **Know your limit.** Set the price you expect to pay for your ad placement and don't go over it.
2. **Know what results you expect from your TV advertising.**
3. **Negotiate.** You don't always want to pay premium prices for your advertising. A good way to find out if you can spend less is by asking the salesperson—after they've told you the rates—when your ad can be shown. If they say immediately, then you can probably negotiate less, if you're willing to wait a few weeks.
4. **The lowest rates can generally be found in the first and third quarters, with January and February (after Christmas) being cheapest of all.**
5. **Always pre-pay your TV advertising.** Don't go into credit with a TV station. You may end up losing track of your costs and spending much more than you originally budgeted for.

5 Questions to Ask Yourself before Finalizing Your TV Budget

THE FIRST THING you need to do is determine exactly how much money you're willing to spend on creating a TV ad. Most of your costs will come from producing and airing the ad itself. Before you finalize your budget, ask yourself the following questions:

1. How elaborate do you want the ad to be?
2. How long do you want it to be? Thirty seconds? Forty-five seconds?
3. How many times do you want it to be shown?
4. What time, and during what show, do you want your ad to run?
5. Will you outsource the production of the commercial?

    While this book is all about doing it yourself, this is definitely an exception. In most cases I advise you to hire someone to produce your commercial. While the costs may seem high, the time and resources it'll take to do it yourself will generally end up being even higher. More importantly, you want your ad to be as good as possible. If you don't have a background in advertising or production, you may just end up hurting your business by making an ineffective or annoying commercial.

Many TV stations have an in-house production team that will write, shoot, and edit your commercial. Some production companies will tell you that doing this isn't standard practice or TV stations generally only work with production companies. This, of course, isn't true! Do your homework. Find out which TV stations have their own production companies, and compare rates and expertise!

If you're on an extremely tight budget, you may even want to think about a still-picture commercial. These commercials contain high-resolution pictures instead of filmed video footage, and can be produced for as little as $100 to $200. These are the "brought to you by" ads that follow the weather or newsbreaks. They're very effective because they grab the audience when they're still sitting in front of the TV, before or after a longer commercial break.

If your commercial has actors in it, you should be given the final sign-off on the actors chosen. You know your business best and should have the final say in who becomes its public face. Make sure to be on set during filming. Major changes are often made to the script during production, and you need to make sure these changes don't alter the primary message in your ad.

Make a Good Offer to the Customer

BEFORE YOU MAKE your commercial, you need to make sure you're actually offering something valuable to the customer through your advertisement. If the ad is not clear or the messaging is not accurate or defined, then you are basically creating a vanity ad for your own purposes and not potential customers, which isn't advisable unless you have a massive advertising budget.

For a commercial, a regular offer isn't enough—your offer needs to be something more than that, something that will stand out from all the other commercials out there sharing the advertising space with you. If you're an electronics store with a backload of outdated computers, don't advertise them as a good offer—it just makes your business look cheap, like it's looking to pawn off unwanted goods.

A good offer would be a discount for the first hundred people who buy the newest version of your flagship electronic item. Other good offers might include a free trial period or consultation, like a free software trial or yoga lesson, which will hopefully turn into a retained customer later on.

Treat the Customer as a Friend

CONSUMERS ARE SUSPICIOUS of advertising, so don't give them any more reason to distrust your TV commercial. Be truthful and avoid false statements, regardless of how good they sound. Platitudes and clichés are sure to resonate badly with your consumer base, so avoid them like the plague. Tricking or patronizing your audience will also reflect badly on you. Treat your audience the way you would a friend—they deserve your respect and honesty. Using trickery, subterfuge, or patronizing comments is treating your customer base like the enemy.

Think of the most annoying TV commercials you've heard lately. There's a good chance that these commercials are annoying, patronizing, or had misleading statements. Why would you want your advertisement to be anything like that?

Give Your TV Commercial a Human Touch

PEOPLE ARE MORE interested in other people than they are in objects or services. Instead of putting the spotlight solely on your product, take the time to highlight the people who make your company special by doing the work they're so great at. This doesn't mean stiff employees staring at the camera in a group shot, it means capturing them in the midst of their job that helped generate your special product.

Take this further, and focus on workers that will appeal to your target audience. If the majority of your customers are women, show your female employees at work.

Find an Angle for Your Commercial

PLAY TO YOUR business's strengths when making your commercial. What are you offering, a physical product or a service? Do you solve a problem, and, if so, is it professional (e.g., Internet security) or personal (e.g., weight loss)?

4 ANGLES YOU SHOULD CONSIDER FOR YOUR AD

1. **Arouse curiosity.** You want the audience to be craving more information. Effective ways to do this include asking a rhetorical question, providing a bit of content that previews valuable information, and stating that you have an exciting new product. For example, "Our new marketing strategy will make you millions."

2. **Arouse an emotional response.** You want the audience to feel empathy during your commercial. This type of ad often draws on people's insecurities and desire for a positive response. It can also draw on the audience's values, and is often used by non-profit organizations for generating donations. For example, "Are you tired of being single in the city?" or "Isn't this child's education worth $5 a month?"

3. **Label yourself a problem solver.** Outline a problem and follow it up by describing how your business can solve it. These problems can be personal or corporate. For example, "Are you too busy to make a healthy dinner?" or "Is your company paying too much for your IT provider?"

4. **Tout your product's success.** If your business or product does something amazing, advertise it. This type of ad is all about the wow factor. You want the audience to be impressed with your business. For example, "Named the best Mexican restaurant in the city by your local newspaper."

Sometimes Less Is More

YOU MAY HAVE tons of products you want to show off in your commercial, but beware of overloading your audience. Remember, consumers can only take in so much imagery in thirty seconds. Pick the best products you have, and commit more screen time to them. Keep in mind that your TV ad is supposed to have a narrative that convinces people to spend their money on your business. Bombarding them with photos won't accomplish this.

Writing a Script for Your TV Ad

AT THE END of the day, you have only thirty seconds of airtime to get your point across, so your script needs to be efficient. Start by thinking of words and phrases that encapsulate your business. Instead of relying on tired clichés, narrow down what your business is great at and why it's so valuable into a few words. After you have enough phrases, try putting them together in complete sentences. If you have too many phrases, find a way to combine them into a few phrases that incorporate your key strengths.

Make sure your script isn't too long or short for the amount of airtime you'll purchase. Make the sentences short and snappy, and place the best one first. People naturally tune out whenever commercials come on, so you have to work really hard to draw them back in.

The narrative for your TV ad should be both seen and heard. The audio and video must complement each other perfectly. If the audio is describing a new product, make sure the video is showing that product!

However, since you're not making an image ad, you need a call to action. Tell the customer to *buy today!* Tell them where and how they can buy your product. Include any information that will help the customer use your business (e.g., email address, street address, website URL, phone number). That being said, don't be overly aggressive. You don't want to come off as self-serving or desperate, which puts consumers off. You want to *pull*, not *push*, the customer toward your business.

Always place your logo or name carefully in your ad, and use it consistently! Do the same with any colors or other images associated with your business. You want to make sure all your products are presented in harmony with your logo or brand. Ideally, the positive feelings people have about your brand would then transfer to your product. For example, if you have two identical shoes, but you labeled one as Nike and left the other blank, people will automatically assume the Nike shoe is higher quality because it carries their brand name.

DOING RESEARCH AND GETTING FEEDBACK

FIRST, FIND OUT what your competitors are doing well—and not so well—and learn from their ads. Don't be shy about using the elements you like in their campaigns within your own TV ads!

You can also ask your customers for ideas. Involving your customers in the creative process is great for two reasons. Instead of just analyzing and guessing what your target market likes, it makes a lot more sense to ask them directly. Remember to rely on more than just one focus group. This can be useful to get a general idea of what your potential customers are looking for. It will also help generate excitement over your upcoming advertisement and future products.

Email your customers from the list you've wisely created, telling them that you're planning on making a commercial, and ask them what would entice them to buy your product.

Ask for honest feedback from your colleagues, friends, and associates at all levels of the production process, from the idea stage to the final cut. These are the people who know you and your business best. If anyone can provide constructive criticism and advice about what works and what doesn't, it's them.

The TV Broadcast Day

LIKE RADIO, TV broadcast hours are typically divided into different segments based on audiences. The standard segments are as follows.

Early morning: 6:00 a.m. to 9:00am

Daytime: 9:00 a.m. to 4:30 p.m.

Early evening: 4:30 p.m. to 7:00 p.m.

Prime access: 7:00 p.m. to 8:00 p.m.

Primetime: 8:00 p.m. to 11:00 p.m.

Late news: 11:00 p.m. to 11:30 p.m.

Late night: 11:30 p.m. to 1:00 a.m.

Overnight: 1:00 a.m. to 6:00 a.m.

Weekend morning: 8:00 a.m. to 1:00 p.m.

Weekend afternoon: 1:00 p.m. to 7:00 p.m.

How to Schedule Your Advertisement

WHILE YOU MAY wish to advertise in the cheaper time slots, it's important that your advertisement is shown at a time that will maximize your chances for new sales. Airing your ad at 4:00 a.m. may save you 50 percent, but, if no one is watching, you're just wasting money. It's better to spend more for a time slot that you know will reach your intended audience.

If you feel your ad would benefit from being shown at different times throughout the day or you have a product that crosses over numerous demographics, talk to the TV station. They may be able to offer you spots that save you money.

As always, try to find the broadcast hour slot that best matches your product and your target market. A commercial for a children's toy probably shouldn't be broadcast for late-night.

What Will It Cost to Air My Ad?

THE COST FOR airing a commercial will vary enormously based on a number of factors: the channel, time of day, show, length, complexity and design of the commercial, the market you're in, and the number of people that tune in to the channel at the time of the ad.

A modest ad can be produced for a couple thousand dollars and be aired at a quieter time for a few hundred dollars. Those prices will obviously skyrocket for elaborate commercials played during primetime slots.

Track Your Results

ARE YOUR ADS increasing your sales or not? Regardless of what your gut says, be sure you've set up a way to track its results. This may involve having people fill out a form—either in person or online—that asks them how they heard about your business, or making sure you and your employees ask customers how they heard about your business.

If you happen to have more than one advertisement running, ask customers which one they saw. The results may surprise you. Two ads that cost the same amount to produce and air may have wildly different results. Learn from your mistakes and use the knowledge for next time.

3 Ways to Stretch Your TV Ad Dollar

1. **Direct response ads** are often given particular slot times that are cheaper than others. The TV station will probably request that the ad contain a phone number or email address where you can be reached.

2. **0 to 24 spots** are slot requests that guarantee your ad will be aired on specific dates, but at random times over the course of 24 hours.

3. **Overnight slots** mean your ad will be played sometime between midnight to 6:00 a.m. Of course, just because you get a better deal doesn't mean you should accept that your ads will only be played after midnight. Make sure you do what's best for your ad and your business. A better idea is to negotiate the rates for your preferred slot times, then see if you can have any 0 to 24 spots or overnights slots thrown in as well.

Put Your TV Ad on the Internet

IT SHOULD GO without saying, but you should put your commercial on the web. The first place to load it is on your website, preferably where it's easy for casual visitors to watch. This is another way to promote your business to new visitors and keep your website up-to-date and lively. Adding videos also helps with your SEO (search engine optimization).

You should also place your commercial on video sites like YouTube and Vimeo. These websites are hugely popular and a great way for your commercial to gain extra traction. If it's humorous or has an interesting angle, it may even go viral, attracting thousands or even millions of views.

YouTube has the added benefit of allowing you to create click-through annotations. This means you can add a little text box to your video, encouraging people to check out more of your videos or subscribe to your channel.

Creating the Perfect Outdoor Ad: Poster or Billboard

IT'S NOT HIGH-TECH, but a great poster may just be the best way to draw attention to your business. If it's in the right location, it could catch the attention of thousands of people. Because of its immediacy, a poster is a great way to highlight an upcoming event or even an upcoming product, which creates buzz for your company without spending too much time or money.

Not so long ago, poster design was an expensive process. However, the explosion of digital graphics and printing means you can now obtain the services of a talented graphic designer for cheap.

If you would rather design your poster yourself, you should have some working knowledge of Adobe Creative Suite. While you can create a basic poster with a word processor, a graphic design program is the de facto method for poster design. Without it, your poster risks looking cheap and uninspiring, especially when it's placed beside other, professional posters.

What Makes a Perfect Poster?
1. **It's readable.** Avoid complex wording or passive phrases.
2. **It's legible.** Make sure it can be read easily from ten or more feet away.

3. **It's organized.** Even a bit of confusion will lose the reader. Make sure the layout is as intuitive as possible.
4. **It's got space.** Your ad shouldn't be cluttered. Using white space gives the reader pause, making it easier for them to organize the information.

HOW MUCH CONTENT SHOULD YOUR POSTER HAVE?

NOT A LOT! Too much content will confuse the viewer. Remember, you're trying to convey a piece of valuable information.

The perfect graphic, photo, or illustration is the best way to get information across. In marketing, it's worth repeating—a picture really is worth a thousand words. The right graphic will make it easier for you to choose your words.

Then keep the wording short and simple—just a few sentences that supply the basic information (i.e., who, what, where, when, and how). Bullet points, if used stylistically, can do this very well.

Studies show that audiences have only eleven seconds to read your poster before they move on. Plan your poster so it can be read in half that time. Make sure passersby catch the headline, at the very least. Remember, people are exposed to the same ad numerous times. As long as they catch the headline the first time, they'll absorb the rest of the content the second time.

HOW SHOULD YOU CHOOSE YOUR HEADLINE?

MAKE SURE YOUR headline is catchy and short. If you had to use one phrase to attract consumers, what would it be? Use active, strong words. Avoid passive language (e.g., words that end with "ing") or the past tense. Always make sure you test a draft version with colleagues and friends.

HOW SHOULD YOU LAY OUT THE TEXT?

STUDIES SHOW THAT people track wording vertically, from center to top to bottom, and horizontally from left to right. This means that you should prioritize your content in the order illustrated below: top-center, top-left, top-right, bottom-left, bottom-right.

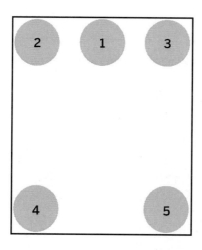

CREATING TEXT

SIMPLE TECHNIQUES THAT you are probably familiar with in any document can be used for poster text. Inserting columns into your poster makes it easier for the reader to follow the direction of information. Your headline should be between 90 and 160 point, bolded. Don't use all capitals—this makes it harder to read. The text of your body should be approximately 35 point.

Where to Place Posters

DIFFERENT COMMUNITIES HAVE different laws about putting up posters. Contact your local city hall before doing any advertising. Many municipalities require you to pay a permit to have your posters advertised. If you don't, the city will tear them down.

When deciding where to place your poster, the busier the better. Place your poster in high-traffic areas. Main streets, intersections, busy stop lights, and commuter stations are all great places that will ensure your poster is seen by a high number of people.

The Perfect Billboard

A BILLBOARD AD needs to be even simpler and more direct than a poster. People driving down a freeway have only around seven seconds on average to view it, so your entire billboard should have only eight to ten words on it. Make sure to include the name of your business and your contact info, plus some directions for finding it (e.g., "Corner of Main and Broadway"). Don't tease your audience like you might in a commercial. You have only a few precious seconds to let them know what they're staring at, so get to the point.

Billboards tend to be very image-heavy. Since you're limited to only a few words, you have to have your image tell the story. Even more than in posters, the headline has to be short and catchy. The text and background colors of your billboard should contrast sharply. Red lettering on an orange background will be hard for drivers to read. Yellow and black colors have proven to be the best at drawing the driver's attention.

3 Rules of Billboard Design

1. **Use ten words or less.** The faster the speed limit, the fewer the words, and the larger they should be.
2. **Don't build your billboard around a direct response.** If you can include your phone number and address, great. But don't be fooled: people are driving, so they don't have time to write down your contact information. Your other marketing campaigns will create a direct response—use billboards as

image-heavy ads for building brand recognition.

3. **Your ad should be clever and clear.** The reader should get a sense of satisfaction from reading it. A billboard that's overly complicated will be lost on the driver and instantly forgotten.

Creating a Perfect Direct Mail Campaign

DIRECT MAIL IS one of the most effective ways of getting your marketing materials to your customers' doorsteps. Direct mail is very similar to an online landing page in some respects; you want to provide enough information for the consumer to take the next step without losing interest or throwing the piece away.

Direct mail is incredibly effective at reaching a geographic audience. If you're looking to increase foot traffic to your store, a direct mail blast to surrounding neighborhoods should make a noticeable difference.

For our direct mail campaigns, we partner with a third-party company that has a good relationship with the post office. This allows us reduced rates and higher geographic coverage. If you don't want to team up with anyone, call your local or national mail service to see if you can get a deal on bulk deliveries.

4 Best Practices for Direct Mail

1. **Have multiple elements.** Different people like reading different things. Some people enjoy reading letters while some like looking at colorful photos that come with brochures. As a rule of thumb, we recommend using brochures and letters, in conjunction, to maximize readership.

2. **Give people many different ways to respond.** One of the biggest difficulties of direct mail is getting a response. Unlike an online ad, people can't simpy click through to a sales page. To minimize this, I always recommend giving your receipients

multiple ways to respond. Give them a URL to your website, the direct line of your sales center, and a form for them to fill out.

3. **Have a compelling call to action.** Just like any other advertising campaign, having a strong call to action will make the difference between someone taking your offer and throwing your materials in the trash. Don't cheap out with the print quality for direct mail either! You need your colors and images to be bold and crisp to attract attention. Saving a few bucks on printing will cost a lot of conversions later on.

   If you don't have in-house experience, we recommend hiring or contracting a design firm to give your materials a professional sheen. Appearances are everything!

4. **Repeat the most important information.** It's impossible to predict where the reader will actually start reading. Only a small proportion of readers will actually read the entire text. Some will skim the headlines, some might only read half of the first paragraph, and some might just look at the images.

   That's why it's so important to make sure your calls to action are clear and repeated throughout all the elements. Anyone who looks at a section of your materials should have a clear idea of what the offering is and why they should care.

· 9 ·

Public Relations

· · · · · · · · ·

DON'T LISTEN TO those who proclaim "No one reads press releases anymore!" or "The news is all doom and gloom these days!" The truth is that pitching positive stories to the media about your brand should still be a part of your marketing efforts. You just need to make sure you get the attention of the right people in the right way.

To clarify, media relations is the specific act of building a relationship with the media to get your story told, and it falls under the general umbrella of public relations (PR).

A well thought-out and eye-catching press release—or news release—is still a fantastic way to get your information to the media in the hope that they'll use it for a story.

Good PR is all in the details. Nailing down the right wording and going after the right contacts will make the difference between success and failure.

Public relations—and its sister, media relations—are powerful tools that every business can use to increase their profile. Today's consumer is constantly plugged into the news and recent events. Newspapers, smartphones, e-readers, blogs, podcasts, and social media sites, like Twitter and Facebook, magnify news stories through horizontal or "viral" communication. In short, the consumer is now the medium.

What this means is that small publicity pieces can yield huge results through social media. Better yet, social media is continually attracting the attention of the large, traditional media outlets, like TV and radio networks, and both local and national newspapers.

So, for example, business X has a small piece on its Facebook page that gets a few thousand hits. All of a sudden business X is inundated with emails and Twitter comments, and the city newspaper runs a piece on it. Now business X can sell this publicity to other media outlets, which will help them get even more publicity!

Thriving on Good PR

THE IMPORTANT THINGS to note is businesses *don't* necessarily succeed because their product or service is better than the competition. The difference between a business that's thriving and one that's struggling often comes down to the level of PR. The successful business is the one in all the papers, on TV, on radio, and trending online while their competitors aren't. Even if you have the best product in the world, it doesn't mean anything if your audience doesn't know about it. This is what PR will help you accomplish.

I realize that most businesses don't have the time or resources to engage in every single type of PR campaign. That's why I've done my best to help you decide what type of PR campaign will match your strategy and your business going forward. Media lists, press releases, pitches, interviews, media kits, crisis communications: I'll weigh the benefits of different types of campaigns, then go through them all one by one, helping you structure your PR campaign and increase your business's publicity.

Contacting the media can be hard business. We realize you may not feel comfortable picking up the phone and telling a stranger your story. But telling your own story is *so* important. Remember, the media loves to tell a good story, so give them your best.

It's crucial that you approach the media with the right message. You need to make sure that you're targeting the right media person and delivering a pitch they'll appreciate. In short, make sure you're doing *them* a favor by providing content that you know their audience will love.

Unfortunately, most PR is done incorrectly. That's why 95 percent of pitches are trashed. It's no wonder editors, reporters, and producers are so impatient. However, this also means that you can stand out from the vast majority if you do your PR properly. If you know who and how to pitch, you'll develop great personal relationships with members of the media.

Keep in mind that these stories *aren't* advertisements. They're real news stories that have been picked up and chosen by reporters because they think it presents a good angle on events.

Why do you want media coverage? Do you want to reach audiences across the nation or do you want to focus on a local community? Are you going for a media channel with the most publicity or the one with the most distinct audience? These are questions you need to ask before moving forward. Each media presents its unique set of strengths and obstacles. So before you pick up the phone or email, know who you are calling and what your story will be.

How to Contact the Media

ONCE YOU'VE CHOSEN the best news outlet for your business, you need to decide the best way to contact them. Here are a few pointers to get you thinking about what way is best for your business (and just as importantly, which ones you're most comfortable doing).

News Releases
- **Write like a reporter—don't use "I" except in quotations.**
- **Be clear and effective.** Not everyone has the same vocabulary as you, so avoid using big or complicated words that might confuse your potential customer.
- **Sell your story, not your product.** Journalists don't want a sales pitch; they want a story!
- **Distribute to the editorial staff who will find your release relevant.** You don't want to annoy staff members by sending your content to the wrong people.
- **Avoid exaggerations and hyperboles—they're clichéd and cheesy.** Is your product really "state-of-the-art," "cutting edge" or "groundbreaking"? People have heard these phrases a thousand times, and they don't really mean anything anymore. Keep your news release truthful and modest.
- **Less is more.** Keep your story to two pages at most.

Letters to the Editor
- **Make sure you're contacting the editor who is best aligned with your business.**
- **Don't email on the weekends or at night.** Many editors don't check their email until the morning, so your email may end up being lost in the clutter. The best time to email is midday, either just before or just after lunch (not between noon and 1:00 p.m.).

- **Make it short and personable.** Be friendly and avoid pitching your business too strongly. Remember, the editor needs to feel they're getting a story, not a sales pitch.
- **Reference the editor by name at the outset.** Let them know this isn't a newsletter or an e-blast!
- **Reference a past story run by the paper in your subject line.** This will help distinguish you from the competition.

Phone Call

- **Call the editor or producer one or two days after you've emailed them your letter or press release.**
- **Don't call at the end of the workday.** Journalists have deadlines and hate being interrupted from them.
- **Smile.** It sounds strange, but smiling while calling will make you sound more welcoming.
- **Write out what you want to say beforehand.** This will help you stay on message and cover all your main points.
- **Rehearse your phone call and make sure it doesn't sound too formal.**
- **Introduce yourself right away and ask if now is a good time to talk.** They'll appreciate you asking.
- **Make your pitch short and sweet.** Journalists are very busy people and generally appreciate succinct conversations.

Press Conference

- **Send out an advisory 48 hours before the conference and once again the morning of the conference.**
- **If you want a certain media station to be there early, call them and let them know.** Give them time to prepare and set up for the conference.
- **Mornings are preferable—but not too early, and provide ample coffee.**

- Choose a place that can adequately fit all of the attendees and their equipment.
- Think of visuals and photos ops—talking heads get boring fast.
- Have full media kits available to hand out.
- Know your competition and explain why you're better than them.
- **Make sure your story is press-conference worthy.** Reporters hate showing up for envelope openings. Make it a show, with good visuals and all the key players present.

10 Tips on Media Etiquette

1. When you're pitching, think about their needs, not your own. Is this story interesting? Will their audience think so? If not, what can you do to change that?
2. Don't make the editor or producer do all the work to develop your story. Take control of your story and flesh the right angle out for yourself.
3. Save the product selling for your advertising. Focus on what makes your business unique.
4. Be honest!
5. Be sensitive to deadlines.
6. If you miss a call, call them back immediately. Don't make them wait—they'll find another story to do in the meantime!
7. If you can't do an interview, offer someone else. Interviews are a great way to add personality to your business and to tell your story in your own words. Don't pass up the chance to do one!
8. Be reachable 24/7. Media work late hours and like to be able to reach their sources at anytime.
9. Always follow up. Don't be discouraged if you don't hear back immediately.

10. If a journalist isn't interested in a story, don't be disheartened—and never pitch them the same story twice (they'll consider your email spam, delete it, and have a lower opinion of you). Instead, approach them when a new story develops.

How to Plan Your Media Relations Campaign

1. Always plan your media relations campaign carefully. Don't just randomly send out news releases—make sure it has a purpose to your story. Take advantage of upcoming holidays. Is there a story you can tell for Christmas, Halloween, Easter, or New Year's Eve? What about community events and festivals? Think about how your business and your product relates to these events and how you can tailor a story to them.
2. Keep a calendar of major community events you may want to sponsor. Write down your deadlines for sending out listings, media advisories, and news releases. At Curve we suggest creating a six-month-advanced calendar that reminds you of any events you should be planning for.
3. Start planning your media relations at least six months in advance. While most media don't plan that far in advance, it's good to be prepared so you can send the right pitch at the perfect time while your competitors are still building their story.
4. Monitor trends and popular ideas and try to link them to your own business. When a story breaks that concerns your industry or service, that's a perfect time to pitch a piece about your company to the media. A reporter will be more interested in what you have to say if it's related to a hot and trending topic.

Working with Your Local Media

LET'S BE HONEST. Your news story probably won't be appearing on *Good Morning America*. And that's fine—your news will usually be most relevant to the local media and to audiences that are most likely to use your business. That's why you should concentrate on local newspapers, blogs, and radio and TV networks.

3 Crucial Things to Understand about the Local Media

1. **Market penetration is better with local media.** More and more studies are showing that community newspapers and local blogs are thriving in the current environment. Local media have strong editorial and loyal readers and are more likely to be receptive to your stories, because their editorial teams have not been slashed (unlike the larger, sexier daily and national papers).

   Even though they may not be *People* magazine or the BBC, they're still a media outlet, so make sure to do your research into your own story leads. The same is true for radio and TV— local audiences trust in their local media more, so give them the same respect you would give to a larger station and pitch them quality stories.

2. **Keep the story local.** The best way to entice local media to your story is to keep it local, too. Remember that local consumers want news and pictures of local people they can relate to, not strangers who have no connection to them or their community. You have to give your local newspaper a reason to write the story.

3. **Plan your announcement.** Be sensitive to editorial deadlines. Presenting your news in time for local newspaper deadlines will work in your favor. A good rule of thumb is to present your stories at least two weeks before your event or story should break.

Work Out What Makes a Good Story

I MENTIONED THIS before, but it's worth reiterating: the best way to get your story into the media is to make it newsworthy. Remember, you're selling stories, not advertising. Let the story promote your business. If you want to promote your product directly to consumers, run an advertisement instead. Editors need stories their readers or viewers will find interesting.

Focus on the human-interest angle. People like reading, watching, and hearing about other people (that's what celebrity culture is based on). They want to hear about personal struggles and triumphs. They want the human narrative laid out for them: what influenced people's decisions, the challenges they faced, and how they overcame adversity.

Let's say you have a good idea of what your story should be. You've planned ahead and know what date you'd like to have it released by. You also have a good idea of how to talk to editors, being sensitive to their time and deadlines. Now you need to figure out which media is the best fit for your story.

First, define your target audience. Know your audience's demographics: their age group, gender, income level, neighborhoods, family, and marital status. With Facebook and other social media, it's possible to know your audience's psychographics as well: their activities, interests, hobbies, heroes, and taste in music, movies, TV, and literature is now (somewhat) public knowledge. When targeting new audiences, find consumers whose demographics and psychographics mirror your existing audience.

Then, find media whose interests best match your own. In other words, the media outlet and your business should share the same audience. If you're a sporting goods store, what's the best media outlet to pitch your story to? If you said a sports radio talk show, you nailed it.

Finally, create a contact list with the names of editors. I will show you how to create one of these later on in the chapter, but for now you should know that it's important to create a list of media contacts that are good candidates for future pitches and news releases.

Writing the Story

SO YOU HAVE your story in mind and you know who you want to reach with it. Now comes the fun part—writing it. A good news release covers all the details of your story and includes contact information. A great news release does those things *and* is so well written that it reads like a newspaper article.

When writing, think of the *story*, not the product. If your pitch has a great storyline and is well written, your story will be more likely to be picked up—in fact, a media outlet may even print it verbatim! This is invaluable, as it allows you to be sure sure your message is being told just as you intended.

Keep your article short and sweet (under 500 words) and try to end it off with five to ten problem-solving tips.

A 4-Step Outline for an Article

FOLLOWING THESE FOUR steps will help you create an effective article.

1. **Tell a personal story that highlights an issue your audience cares about.** Why did you get into the business? What goal were you hoping to achieve? What's the problem that relates to you *and* to your audience?

    Example of a problem: The owner of one restaurant was dismayed with the lack of "authentic" Italian pizzerias in her town. She remembered the great pizzas she had enjoyed on her travels in Sicily.

2. **Describe how you discovered the solution.** How does your business solve the problem for your customer? Describe the catalyst, the "Aha!" moment. Refrain from selling your business explicitly; instead, tell the story of how you discovered the solution. Let the reader connect the dots between your business and you.

   Example of a solution: The owner realized that an authentic Italian pizzeria could bring "real Sicilian pizza" to her town and provide variety in a stale market. People who wanted "real" pizza wouldn't have to travel to Italy but could experience it in their own backyard.

3. **List the specific benefits of your solution.** Again, you don't need to sell your business explicitly. Don't say "your business" or "your product"—rather, talk about "the ideal product." The consumer can connect the dots and realize that your business is the answer to their prayers. Doing this makes your story seem more objective and less like a sales pitch.

   Example of benefits: The owner of the pizzeria lists how a great authentic pizza should be made: thin crust, fresh sauce made from organic tomatoes, fresh garden-grown basil, wood-fired oven, pairing the pizza with the perfect glass of wine, etc.

4. **Give the solution in a series of simple steps.** Contemporary audiences are skeptical buyers who are wary of being duped or lied to, so telling them the specific benefits of one solution may not be enough. They want you to *prove* that you've found a solution. Your job is to prove that your solution really works (without giving away anything to your competition). By listing the steps you increase the perceived objectivity and authenticity of your story.

   Example of steps: The pizzeria uses a wood-burning stove that she had shipped over from Sicily, not an inferior conveyor heater like the competition. She uses fewer ingredients and hand picks them herself to make sure she only uses the best.

The owner is knowledgeable in wine pairings for each type of pizza. The owner romantically describes her time in Sicily, learning how to make the perfect pizza and sampling the local wines.

Answer the 5 W's

MAKE SURE YOUR news release answers the five W's about your story: who, what, when, where, and why. Here are some questions you should ask yourself *before* you write your news release:

- Who is involved? Who is contacting the reporter?
- Who should the reporter contact for more information?
- Who would this news appeal to?
- What's the story?
- When is it happening (include time and date if it's an event)?
- Where is it happening?
- Why is this story happening now? Why are you contacting this reporter about it?

You would be shocked at how many reporters say they've received news release pitches that have left out basic information, such as who to contact for more information, their phone number, and the business's website!

Writing a News Story for Your Company

IF YOU KNOW how to write a strong newspaper story, you can attempt to write your own articles for your local paper. Many newspapers have sections dedicated to guest columnists. Such a column allows you to write your story in your own words, so you'll know the important parts of your message aren't glossed over or ignored by the journalist.

Contact your local newspapers to see if they have any sections coming up that might be relevant to your business, and ask if they'd be interested in having you write a guest column.

A popular type of paper article is the "problem-solver." These articles educate the reader on how to solve a common problem on their own. This also works great with popular local blogs.

HOW TO CREATE A PROBLEM-SOLVING PITCH

1. Pick your topic, create a brief introduction, and then list a series of problem-solving tips.
2. Unlike traditional pitches, these are aimed at solving a distinct problem the readership has instead of telling a story.
3. The points must be short and to the point and contain valuable content (unlike ads!).
4. Make sure they're interesting and fun!
5. If the reader wants to know more, they can Google your name or business.
6. Email your problem-solving article to magazines, newsletters, and newspapers for greater coverage.

5 DIFFERENT TYPES OF ARTICLES

DON'T PIGEONHOLE YOURSELF into creating just one type of article. Explore these different types of articles and try your hand at something new!

1. **"How-to" articles:** These are practical guides that give your audience detailed instructions on how to solve a particular problem. Many include step-by-step instructions.

   Examples: How to set up a Facebook page; how to make the perfect chocolate cake; how to choose your first car.
2. **Hot tip lists:** An all-time favorite! People love lists. How many magazine covers do you see with the phrase "Top 10" in them? Listings and rankings always perk consumers' interests. People love to have things categorized for them, to simplify their decision-making. Top 10 restaurants? Bars? Phones? Flat-screen TVs? Hockey players? Lists—especially rankings—are a great way to get published.

The number of entries in your list and the style will depend on your industry and your topic. Things that are more time-intensive generally have fewer tips. Likewise, lists that require more information have fewer entries, whereas lists that require little explanation can be much longer. Rankings usually run from first to last.

Examples: "Top 10 ways to get new customers," "Top 10 tips for having a strong Twitter presence, " "The 3 most important ways to keep your customers coming back for more."

3. **Industry news articles:** These releases are great when your business has experienced a positive change. You can write them for customers to highlight recently released products or when hosting an event. You can write them for internal audience, such as shareholders and owners when there's a joint venture or a merger or before an initial public offering (IPO).

   Examples: New products, new distribution service, new location for purchasing product, new destination for airline, new discount on product, joint merger between two companies and new ownership.

4. **Interview articles:** These are great when you hire a new employee, get a great review from a customer, or get a recommendation from an expert or public figure.

   Examples: Interview satisfied customers (especially if they happen to be well-known), an employee who has received an accolade, an expert related to your industry who endorses your business, or a new employee who brings new skills to your business.

5. **Product articles:** Let your product tell the story. Use this type of article to describe a product or service from the point of view of the customer. Focus on how your product benefits the consumer.

   Examples: Updates or enhancements on current products, new product releases, reviews of products, and any deals or discounts on current products.

Analyze each type of article and decide whether it can help create publicity for your business. What's your company currently doing? Has it recently expanded its operations or released a new product? Has a celebrity or public figure endorsed your product? Has someone on your team been recognized for their work? Find the angles and use them! Not only will you increase your publicity—you'll also have more content to keep your website updated!

Writing a Press (News) Release

A WELL-WRITTEN PRESS release can generate a high amount of interest from media outlets and be key in providing free media coverage for the client. If you're not a confident writer, there are many freelancers you can find through online sites that can follow the structure below.

While there's no one way to write a press release, it should best represent your story, product, and business. Your objective is to convince the media outlet that you have a story to tell that will be of interest to their audience.

Sometimes an unformatted email a couple of paragraphs long can be even more effective than one with a lot of formatting. The most important thing is to make sure that your story comes through. Don't let the format or the rules bury a great story or a great piece of writing!

Creating a Press Kit

IF YOU'RE PLANNING on doing your own public relations, you need to have a package called a press kit always at the ready. Your press releases (inspired by the examples above) will be a key part of the kit.

A press kit (also known as a media kit) is a pre-packaged set of promotional materials that a business, person, or organization uses alongside an announcement to boost it. Press kits were originally only used by big corporations, but nowadays every business should have one on hand because you can host them on your website or print and email them out if necessary. A strong press kit increases your brand recognition, raises awareness, and helps build a reputation for your business.

Think of your press kit as your company's curriculum vitae. They're collections of information that best present your business. News articles, press releases, logos, fact sheets, and reviews are all appropriate materials. A good press kit should generate interest from the people you hope to work with, whether direct connections (consumers, clients, and investors) or indirect connections (media outlets and new employees). Make sure your press kit is enticing and represents the biggest strengths of your business. The goal here is to impress your readers so they want to know more about your business. Your press kit should include the following:

- **A pitch letter:** Tell the reader within the first three sentences why your business relates to them and why they should care about what you have to say.
- **Business cards:** Never insert just one business card; you want them to pass your cards along to colleagues and associates.
- **Recent articles:** The recency of an article is important because it'll add more weight to any of the facts and claims inside the article for the reporter reading it.
- **Audio and video files:** Include a link to any video or audio you may have produced. B-roll for TV is general video of your business operations, such as a profile of the operations or story of the owner. Place all of this high-resolution material on YouTube or Vimeo for easy viewing and download.
- **Photos:** Get a few good shots of owners, product lines, storefront, operations, and other key staff.

- **Bio sheet:** Create a short biography about the business and the key team players.
- **Frequently asked questions:** Include a list of common questions your business receives and their answers.

Once you have your press kit and material collected, you need to print copies to have available when necessary and place digital versions on your website:

Creating a Media List

A MEDIA LIST is a catalogue of media outlets, including individuals, departments, and companies, which you either create yourself or purchase. Compile your own list in an Excel spreadsheet. Include every contact's first and last name, associated media outlet, title (editor, publisher, journalist, etc.), and a brief description of their professional expertise.

While detailing such information may seem unnecessary, remember that you may need to contact these sources on many occasions for future releases. It'll also allow someone else to use your list without consulting you. Furthermore, knowing a bit of personal information about each contact lets you tailor each email to the contact's interests and expertise.

You can buy media lists or subscribe to lists, but if you're focusing on local media, it should not be too difficult to track down the key players you need to know. For more sophisticated and far-reaching campaigns, you may want to check online for service providers.

Setting up a Google Alert for certain subjects is a great way to find reporters who cover news in your industry. A Google Alert is a free notification service from Google. You can tell Google to track certain keywords. Anytime there's a new mention of the keyword, they'll send you an email with all the details and a link. This can help you keep track of anyone talking about or mentioning your topic on the Internet. When it comes to building your Google Alerts, the trick is to not make your subject too general or too specific.

Pitching to Media Contacts

WHILE DOING A massive email blast to thousands of reporters might be appealing, your story will be lost in the ton of pitches most reporters receive every day.

While labor intensive, the best way to pitch media is by making direct contact with a specific reporter. You should research someone in advance to find out who you think will love your story.

The best way to attract the attention of individual reporters is by referencing a work they have done by inserting it into the subject line.

Referencing other articles a media outlet or journalist has produced sets you apart from everyone else and gets you noticed. It shows that you're not just mindlessly sending out an e-blast but have done your research.

Citing the previous work of a reporter also makes your story less risky to promote. Instead of being a brand new and untested idea, you have connected it to one of the stories they have already run in the past. This makes your story "safer" to run, so to speak.

While all this research may seem time-consuming, basic search engine tips make finding articles fast. Most media outlets also have their own search engines embedded in their websites, so it's easy to search by journalist's name or your topic to find articles related to your pitch.

The Phone Pitch: Following up with Journalists

SO YOU'VE CREATED your media contact list and sent out your amazing press release. Now you sit back and wait for the phone calls, right?

Wrong! If you just send out your email it may never get opened, let alone looked at. Again, journalists are extremely busy and have little to no patience. They receive hundreds of emails a day and are prone to deleting anything that looks like spam. So if you don't follow up on your press release, it may never get a fair chance.

In short, you're going to have to pick up the phone and pitch your story *yourself.*

Wait two days after sending out your press release before following up with a phone call. That is enough time for the editor to go through his or her emails.

How to Make the Phone Call

PEOPLE MAKE CAREERS just out of phone techniques. I have had calls from great salespeople and terrible ones. Pitching and talking to media is no different. It's a kind of sales, but in this case you may only have one chance to close the sale, especially since fewer and fewer reporters or editors pick up their phones these days. So, before you grab the phone, prepare yourself.

First, write down what you're going to say. Make your pitch 30 seconds or less. You don't want to leave anything important out, but you don't want it to drag on. Make it sound unscripted. You're looking to be efficient with your words, but you don't want it to read like bullet points. Find a middle ground and let your words flow in a conversational tone.

Second, practice, practice, practice. Read your pitch out loud to see if comes across as natural, making sure to time it. Cut it down if it feels too long. If you really don't think you can remove anything out without compromising your story, so be it: leave it in.

Everyone who pitches talks too fast. Talk slower than you think you should and maintain that pace throughout. Trust me—you'll come across as more professional and be easier to understand.

Practice with an audience and ask for feedback. Is it too long? Not long enough? Does it sound natural? Does it grab you? It's better that your co-workers and friends point out your mistakes instead of the editors.

Third, before you call get your information right. Call the right person. It sounds obvious, but always do your research and make sure you're contacting someone from the right department. Calling the travel writer about your new beer launch will make you an embarrassment.

Know the right times to call. If possible, get to know a media outlet's publication dates, story meeting times, and shift times. A good rule of thumb is to only call between 10:00 and 11:30 or between 1:00 and 4:00. If you're calling on a Monday, you may want to wait until 10:30 or 11:00. Reporters are often buried with emails on Monday mornings and will be too busy catching up to listen to your pitch or even pick up the phone!

Fourth, start by introducing yourself. Ask if now is a good time to talk. As I mentioned before, reporters appreciate it when you value their time and are more likely to listen to your pitch if you don't force it on them. If they're busy, ask them if there's a convenient time to talk.

Get to the point immediately. Don't jump around the point or hype it up too much. Tell them your business, your reason for calling (you have a great story), and why *they* are the perfect person for it.

Explain your story in less than 30 seconds. Why is it newsworthy, how does it relate to the media outlet, and, most importantly, why would their audience find the story interesting? If applicable, make sure to mention how the story is relevant to current events or trends.

Explain the "brass tacks" of the story. What does it involve? Is it an event? A new product? Are you inviting the media to a launch? Time? Location? Photos? Interview? Be ready to provide all the details.

Don't repeat your press release verbatim. Add your personality to the pitch and make sure you're saying something extra or better than the info in the press release (which they may even have read).

Keep going back to why your story is newsworthy. Always look at the value of your pitch from the journalist's point of view.

And finally, close the deal. Ask the reporter if they're on a deadline. It lets them know you appreciate their time and are willing to work within their timeline, not yours.

Offer exclusivity. Let the reporter know that you won't approach the paper's competitors if they decide to write about you.

Go off the record only to provide background about your business they wouldn't hear—or read—otherwise. This helps create a relationship and a level of respect with the reporter, because they feel you aren't hiding anything from them. But be very careful and say upfront that what you're about to say is off the record. If you're not comfortable or worry it's confidential information that should not be released, then don't go off the record.

Things You Should *Not* Do

OF COURSE, THERE are some things you should *not* do, and it is often surprising how many people actually tell the reporter how they should cover the story. It's their job to present great stories. Giving them advice on their trade is a surefire way *not* to get your story or any future story covered.

Never ask to see the story before it goes to print or air. Remember, these people are extremely busy, and the idea of catering to your needs is enough to dissuade them from telling your story.

Or tell them how your story would be a "refreshing" change from their usual stories, or how one of their colleague's recent stories wasn't to your liking.

Or act like you're doing them a favor by providing free story ideas.

Or that you're planning on pitching your story to other media outlets (even if you add that their outlet is your first choice).

Or lie. Always be truthful when talking to the press. If you don't know the answer to something, say that. And then tell them you'll get back to them later. But make sure you do get back to them.

Things You *Should* Definitely Do!

BE PERSISTENT WITHOUT being bothersome. While being tenacious helps, you don't want to get a reputation for badgering the media. All news outlets have unpredictable schedules and finite editorial space and give precedence to breaking news or late ad bookings, so don't be surprised if it takes longer than expected for your story to be released.

Help the journalists cover the story. Ask them when they need content, what their deadlines are, whether they would like photos emailed to them, and so on. Your job is to help facilitate the story coverage. You can help in many ways, whether by providing contacts or facilitating with interviews.

Interviews and Speeches

"WILL THE MEDIA *want to interview me after I send them my press release?*"

Surprisingly, journalists and editors frequently don't need to interview you after they decide to tell your story. A well-written press release often answers all the questions they may have. You may find that they ask you to answer a couple of additional questions via email, but that's often it. If a journalist does want to talk, it'll usually be over the phone.

If you do get an interview request, be prepared to answer any sort of question. Take the time to get familiar with the show or publication and know a bit about the reporter or interviewer. Make sure you know the topic of the story and what angle they might be going for. Have a few interesting facts, points, or quotes ready to use. Don't memorize all of your answers or you'll come across as mechanical and formal.

5 Things to Avoid during the Interview

1. Don't say anything that you wouldn't be happy to see in print or hear on TV or the radio.
2. If you don't have an answer to a question, tell the reporter you'll get back to them at a later date. Don't make answers up!
3. Don't say anything "off the record," unless it's background information. It makes you look immoral.
4. Never assume at any point that the interviewer is speaking "off the record." Anything you say may be printed. Reporters are waiting for you to drop your guard!
5. If a reporter gets aggressive or insulting, don't take it personally. Reporters are generally very professional, so this will probably never happen, but if it does, politely answer their questions and end the interview.

Photography for the Media

IN MARKETING, A picture really is worth a thousand words. Photographs are amazing at telling your story and attracting an audience to your brand.

It can't be overstated how much more appealing your story will be to the media if you attach a few high-resolution shots. TV and print media love to add "color" to a story with images. Make their job easier for them!

You should always have photos ready to add to a press release. If you don't, plan to have them ready soon and make sure to tell the media outlet that photos are available upon request. Journalists are often more open to your pitch if you say you have high-resolution photos ready for them to use, and readers are much more likely to notice your article if it has a great photo with it.

Some media outlets have photographers on the payroll that they send out to take professional photographs. Outlets with smaller budgets, like most community papers, accept amateur photographs and will be happy to use photographs you provide. Being able to supply rights-free images will help you with all but the largest media outlets.

Do I Need to Hire a Professional Photographer?

HIRING SOMEONE TO take professional photographs may be worth the money to ensure you're getting your best possible image out to the public. This is one area where skimping isn't advised.

The great thing about investing in photographs is that you then use them for all your marketing campaigns for months or even years to come. Websites, posters, news articles, interviews, media kits, and other promotional materials all look better when they feature stunning photographs. Even years after the event or campaign, you can use the photo as part of a case study on your website to show all your new clients what your company has achieved.

10 Photo Tips

1. **Take exciting and colorful shots and avoid clichés and boring setups.** Ribbon-cuttings and handshakes are boring. Your photo says everything about your business—a bad or a boring photo is worse than having none at all.

2. **Take the photos twice as close to the subject as you think you should.** Photos in newspapers or magazines may be reproduced quite small, so make sure you've got close-ups in high resolution.

3. **Make sure the light is behind the photographer, not the subject.**

4. **If you can't provide an action shot, provide a headshot of the business owner or a photo of the entire team.** If you use a team shot, be sure to have them at a good size. A tiny image will cause issues in newsprint.

5. **When working with local or community media, try to get your face in the news.** A local, familiar face can really resonate with consumers.

6. **Some newspapers run great photos or have a "photo of the day" section with no story attached.** Ask your local newspapers about such opportunities and always have a great photo in stock. This will get your business more visibility and help you build up your relationship with your media contact.

7. **When you send the photo, always include a brief cutline** (e.g., "John Doe Opens up Newest Store in Yaletown"), along with the date and the photographer's name.

8. **The caption and photo headline should clearly and concisely answer the five W's** (i.e., who, what, where, when, and why).

9. **Make sure you attach a photo credit for copyright purposes.**
10. **Be sure to send the photo in the proper format** (e.g., JPEG, GIF, etc.) and file size the media outlet prefers. Ask the reporter for details before sending any photos.

Events

HOLDING AN EVENT or launch is a great way to concentrate your marketing budget and maximize the results. Events are easy to control because they have a beginning and a middle (hopefully a glorious celebration with lots of buzz), and then gracefully come to an end. Your event can be as simple as a $2 latte, which is really a gimmick—though we at Curve would treat it as an event—or as big as a street party. It really depends.

Whether your marketing budget is $10,000 or $100,000, we would apply our Buzz Formula to your event or gimmick. The Buzz Formula (30/30/30/10) works best when you have a limited marketing budget. It's all about maximizing your budget by being creative with your advertising, your media partners, and your PR, and then promoting an event, stunt, or gimmick.

Event Listings Websites

IF YOU'RE HOLDING an event such as a party, product release event, or workshop, you should take advantage of free listings websites to increase your publicity. Some are purely listings websites—perfect for attracting tourists who are looking for fun events—while others, like news and media sites, often have event calendars. The benefit of posting on these sites is that they attract huge traffic. People are already viewing the website for other information, and many of them will click on the event pages. This is either because they're looking for something to do or they're simply curious. Industry magazines and Internet directories may also have event listing pages.

Many event listing sites require you to sign up to place a listing. Make a quick, generic sign-in and password for yourself. You should unclick the box that says you'd like to receive updates, as these will quickly add up and start flooding your email. While it takes a bit longer to create new accounts, the benefit is that your listing will often be published immediately. Other event sites don't require any sign-in, although most of them will vet your listing prior to publishing it.

Bloggers, Tweeters, Facebookers, and Other Local Thought Leaders

DON'T FORGET ABOUT all those people in your community who are becoming celebrities with their own social media presence. They are definitely worth connecting with. Though they may not be multi-million-dollar media channels, these local thought leaders are now *crucial* in getting local coverage. People follow them religiously, and many of them are happy to post your event on their social medium of choice—Twitter, Facebook, Tumblr, a blog, and the list goes on. While not all of them have a calendar listing page, a mention from them will do wonders in increasing your local publicity.

7 Tips for Finding the Best Bloggers

1. Most cities have an annual "Top 10 Blogs " list. Google "best blogs of" Vancouver, Toronto, New York, etc., and nine times out of ten, you'll find that someone has posted a ranking. Many of the more popular subjects will also have their own blog rankings. Restaurant, fashion, and tech blogs are typically ranked annually, so make sure to check to see if your industry has a list of celebrated bloggers available.

2. Google ranks bloggers organically by the amount of content they contain, how regularly they update and post, and the amount of links outsourced, among other factors. The blogs that show up first in your Google search are often the best.

3. See how often a blogger updates. If they post less than twice a week, they're probably not worth reaching out to.

4. Many blogs have a "search" bar. Use it to see if the blogger writes regularly about events or businesses in your community. A locally based blogger that regularly posts about businesses in one town is more likely to have followers in that same town only.

5. The best bloggers also regularly post content on Twitter and Facebook. Check out their pages and see how many followers or "likes" they have and how regularly they update these social media sites.

6. Popular bloggers tend to have sponsoring opportunities. If the blog you're looking at has that option, it's a safe bet that they're quite popular.

7. There are free SEO software programs that show you how many people are visiting a website from a Google search. SEO Quake is a great free program that places a bar above every site. It provides a page rank as well as the average amount of people that visit the site through Google searches every month. Generally speaking, any blog that has a page rank of less than three is below average. Download the software program at seoquake .com to see how blogs you manage or ones you follow rank.

Media Advisories

A MEDIA ADVISORY alerts editors to an upcoming event in the hope that they'll send a reporter to cover it. It contains basic information on what the event is, who's holding it, and when it's happening. An advisory should catch the editor's attention by making your event sound interesting enough to justify staff coverage (see the sample on the next page).

Using your contact list, email your advisory to your community newspaper *three weeks before* your event, and to TV, radio, and daily newspapers (if appropriate) *two weeks* ahead. Phone

a day or two later to make sure the advisory arrived. As the
event gets closer, follow up with news releases or phone calls
to remind the media that it's happening and to see if they plan
to come out for it.

SAMPLE MEDIA ADVISORY

Attention-Grabbing Headline that Sums up your Story Concisely (and that can also be used in our email subject line)
Name of City, State—Summary of your event including the
title, location, and times. One sentence about what the event
is and why people should attend. For more information about
the event, visit www.yourwebsiteaddress.com.

WHAT: Title of event, promotion

WHO: Name and title of who will be there, so reporters know
who to speak to (the spokesperson, talent, or host of your
event)

WHEN: Date

TIME: Times

LOCATION: Location, address

TICKETS: Pricing or special instructions if applicable

About Your Business

Short summary of your company/organization/group, including when and why it was founded, what product or service
you provide, etc.

Reference:

YOUR NAME

YOUR COMPANY

T: ###-###-#### ext. #

C: ###-###-####

E: yourname@youremail.com

Twitter, Facebook, and other social media contacts

Sponsoring an Event

SPONSORING AN EVENT is a great way to increase your public profile in the community. It involves providing cash or an in-kind fee paid to an event or organization in return for access to promotion and publicity. It's a very effective way to increase your profile within the community and media.

You may want to reserve a portion of your marketing budget for sponsorship opportunities. Some companies also set aside a product or gift every year to donate to various organizations or set up an annual scholarship for a local high school student. Find a solution that works well for you.

7 Ways to Make Sure Your Event Runs Smoothly

1. Make sure everyone on the guest list has been invited!
2. When making a guest list, include everyone's name, "plus ones," contact information, and the media outlet they're affiliated with.
3. Create an attractive e-invitation. These are quite easy to do using any email template platform, like MailChimp or Constant Contact. Find a template that works for you and edit it as necessary for your needs.
4. Send out follow-up emails after sending out the invitation, and be sure to ask people to RSVP.
5. If your local media has agreed to send a reporter to cover your event, make sure to assign someone to greet them, show them around, and help them in any way possible.
6. If you're not hosting the event but are working or volunteering for it, support the host in making choices like the venue, the food, the drinks, the music, etc.
7. Make sure the party goes smoothly, using volunteers and paid staff so the hosts can relax and connect with their guests.

The cost of sponsoring an event varies greatly but is usually dependent on the following main factors.

What's the size of the event or organization? Generally speaking, the more popular the event, the more expensive it'll be for you to sponsor it. A music festival that draws 50,000 people is a much more attractive sponsorship opportunity than one that attracts only 5,000.

What type of audience will it attract? You want to get more people to spend their money on your business, so sponsoring events that attract a high-income audience is something you need to consider. What type of people will be going to the event? What's their socio-economic background? If the event is for children, will their parents also be attending? Make sure the event audience is able and willing to purchase your product.

Where is the event taking place? Where does your consumer base live? Can the people attending the event use your business, or are they too far away to be realistic? And what's the average income level of the people in the area? If the event is unlikely to attract people outside the community, make sure the locals can afford your business!

Will there be advertising before the event? Many events do little to no advertising beforehand. This is especially true for free community events that take place annually. This may not affect turnout, but it'll limit the exposure that you as the sponsor gets.

Before agreeing to sponsor an event, ask whether or not your business will be publicized in pamphlets and newspapers and on radio and TV. You could find out you're paying a huge sum of money to just have your name on a banner the day of the event. It's much better to sponsor events that advertise weeks or even months ahead and will attach your name to the title. Ask also how your business will be written alongside the event. Typically you want it look as if it's *your* event, rather than one paid for by you. You want to make it look like your business has organized the entire event.

While it may look like philanthropy to the community, sponsorship definitely has a commercial objective to heighten your company's visibility. It's a win-win situation. Your company gets the exposure it wants, and different organizations get the funds they need.

Sponsorship provides an opportunity for publicity. Interviews and news stories often spring forth from these events without any extra effort or money!

Sponsoring the right event or organization can shape consumers' attitudes toward your company. Sponsoring an artistic, environmental, or children's event gives the impression that you hold these things in the utmost regard. Ask yourself what the event you're considering to sponsor says about your company. What perceived attributes of the event do you want for your business? Sponsoring community events can solidify your brand image as someone who cares about the neighborhood.

On the flip side, sponsoring unpopular or controversial businesses and organizations can have the reverse effect on your company. Does the event have any legal problems? The last thing you want to do is associate your business with controversy. Do your research and make sure the event is popular in the community.

Organizing events is both time- and resource-intensive, so, for PR purposes, you may want to link yourself with an event being hosted by another organization. If the local Boys and Girls Club is celebrating its twenty-fifth anniversary this year, you could contact them and offer to donate cash or gifts for the festivities.

When deciding what events to sponsor, keep your company's corporate philosophy in mind. Look for events or organizations that can strongly relate to your philosophy.

Even if you're sponsoring a non-profit event or organization, sponsorship shouldn't be confused with philanthropy. Philanthropy is supporting a cause without any commercial incentive. Companies use sponsorship to achieve commercial objectives, such as increased visibility, brand recognition, increased sales, and brand trust.

Promotions

MAKE THE MOST out of your donations or sponsorship. Don't just rely on the organization's event manager to promote your donation to the media—take the time to contact the local newspaper yourself to set up a photo shoot and tell them about the story. This is your sponsorship, so you need to take control and make sure you get the most out of your dollars.

If you're the one hosting an event, you may want to consider selling sponsorship to your media. These "value-added promotions" help round out your advertising campaign, and if you're making a significant ad buy with a media outlet, you should expect to get some form of promotion with your buy (e.g., free newspaper or radio publicity).

You should expect an even stronger promotion if you have granted the media sponsor the title sponsorship of your event. This works well for retail and some consumer products. The media outlet may also let you access their VIP list if you're launching a product or company.

40 Ways to Promote Your Assets

WHEN PLANNING A PR campaign, it's often difficult to think of a story angle. Many businesses have great stories just waiting to be told. These questions will get your creative juices flowing and help you think of the perfect story angle for your business.

- Is your business doing something amazing at a trade show?
- Can you show off your product to someone who has never heard of you?
- Has your company evolved? If so, can you display this evolution in some tangible way?
- Is there a trending regional or national news topic that you can tie to a free giveaway? Think of annual events!
- Can you associate your product with a certain holiday or season?
- Is there a financial or economic trend your business can utilize? Is your product less expensive or more efficient than your competitors?
- Do you have a life story or childhood event that you can lend to your business to give it a human element? Financial, health, and emotional issues can really help tell a story.
- Do you have any associations with schools in the area?
- Do you experience more business during certain weather conditions?
- Does your business do charity or pro bono work?
- Do you have a specific issue or handicap that you overcame to perform your job?
- Do any celebrities or public figures use your product or business?
- When is your next anniversary?
- Do any of your co-workers have personal stories that represent your business?
- Have any of your employees gone beyond the call of duty to serve a customer? Have you received any positive reviews that you're comfortable sharing?
- Do you have an expertise in a certain field? Do people ask you for your advice?
- What are your other interests or hobbies? Can they help tell a story?

- Do you have a new product, or are you upgrading an existing product or service?
- Do any of your vendors have monthly or bi-monthly publications? If so, could you promote your business in their magazine?
- Does your work involve assisting the less fortunate?
- Do media outlets frequently cover your type of business?
- Is one of your clients a famous company?
- Has your company undergone changes in customer policies or in distribution methods?
- Is your company closing in on a record?
- Have you worked or donated to non-profit organizations?
- Is your company diversifying its operations?
- Do you have any free tips you can give to people in your industry on how to save money?
- Do you have an impressive statistic or figure that's worth publicizing?
- Is your industry currently undergoing a trend or change? Can you comment on this?
- Are there new laws being enacted that affect your operations?
- Is your business used at a well-known event?
- Can you survey your consumers or people in your industry?
- What charities or non-profits do you support, either financially or creatively?
- Would your business story be interesting to people from your childhood community?
- Has your business been visited by a celebrity or public figure?
- Have you completely changed your business plan?
- Do you have bold predictions about the future of your business?
- Do you or an employee work at a charitable or non-profit organization?

- Are you planning a major sale?
- Does your business location hold any special interest or history in the community?

Measuring Your PR Results: Google Alerts

GOOGLE ALERTS ISN'T just great for finding media contacts and stories—you can also use it to track any publicity. You can pay large firms a lot of money to track every time you're mentioned in the media, but Google allows you to essentially do the same thing for free! Just go to google.com/alerts to track keywords or phrases about you in the media.

To do this, you must:

- Set up a free account with Google.
- Input two or three different word combinations, such as your brand, your product, or your company's name.
- Watch and wait. Google will do a daily or weekly search of all results and inform you if you've been mentioned in the media. Not only does Google Alerts track media hits, it also shows you where you're being discussed online.

You can also set up Google Alerts for your phone number, your name, your business, and your website. After being interviewed or pitching your press release, you should set up an alert so you'll know when a reporter has written about you. Make sure to quickly promote any PR you get on your website. Reviews are great pieces of advertising that you need to publicize!

Oddly enough, reporters often write a story based on your press release and never get around to letting you know! You'll want to use these articles on your website and in other promotional items. Use Google Alerts to keep track of any mentions of your business.

Research PR Campaigns to Improve Your Skills

ONE OF THE best ways to improve your PR is to follow and learn from others. Pay close attention to people who are pitching their stories. Newspapers, magazines, radio, and TV are all rich sources of PR tips. If you want to work with a particular magazine or show, follow their work and learn what types of stories they like to tell. Understanding what journalists, producers, and editors think makes a good story will help you construct the perfect custom pitch!

SECTION 4

Taking Stock of Your Marketing Budgets and Plans

IF YOU'VE READ this far, you're now ready to take stock of and work out your detailed marketing budget and plan. But first, you should ask yourself a couple of simple questions: what are your brand's strength and weaknesses, and what should your marketing budget be?

Question 1: What are your brand's strength and weaknesses—and can you handle the growth?

The strengths and weaknesses of your company are two very important things you need to understand before you move forward with any marketing plans. When it comes to strength, ask yourself what your company can do or achieve with its current capabilities. A good example of a strength would be Walmart's distribution channels and organization. Their extreme efficiency in transporting and setting up their products across hundreds and hundreds of stores dramatically cuts their costs. Because of this, they can afford to sell their products at low prices.

If that example was a little intimidating, don't worry. Think local for now: what can your business do that one of your competitors in town can't do? It could be your connections to a supplier, your high-quality products, your connections with the media—anything like that would be considered a strength.

On the other hand, a weakness is something not many companies want to talk about. It's important that you identify your weaknesses as honestly (and bluntly) as possible. Do customers frequently complain about your customer service? Do your products have a history of defects? It's crucial you identify and fix (or at least minimize) these weaknesses before you take your marketing plan forward. This is important because once you enter the public eye (through PR, advertising, or any other efforts), your business will be scrutinized and analyzed like never before.

I have no doubt in my mind that your business will start taking off once you've used the Buzz Formula for yourself, but you need to keep your infrastructure in mind. Put yourselves in the shoes of the $2 latte company. Would your business be ready to expand at that rate? You would need to think about where you would put all the new workload that would come with it. Would you want to hire new staff? Go for some interns or contractors? Each choice comes with its own benefits and costs, and it's important to think about all the implications before you begin.

Question 2: What should my marketing budget be (AKA what can you afford)?

Curve has always believed that a multifaceted marketing campaign will produce the best results. That's why we approach our clients' needs by thinking about every option: the best PR outlets, web design, social media presence, and media buys. In our fifteen-plus years in business, we have worked with enough small businesses to know that they value efficient campaigns that get the most of their dollar.

The devil is in the details, so here's the devil—detailed marketing strategies for businesses tend to have budgets of $10,000, $50,000, and $100,000+. What chunk of your marketing pie should you allocate to your online presence, your advertising strategy, or a PR push? How much of that $5,000 online budget should go to the website and how much toward SEO optimization, PPC, and Google AdWords?

The answers will largely depend on the nature of your business: retail, consumer product, service business, non-profit, or an event, like a concert or a trade show. The key is not to spread your money too thin. Get the basics right—like I suggested for setting up your online presence—and then do your research on what medium your audience can be found in. If you keep your plan to fewer than three mediums—say, online, print, and outdoor—it's more likely you'll stay on budget and have a good return on your investment.

Appendix 1

How to Set up a Successful WordPress Site for Your Business

* * * * * * * *

Step #l: Purchase a Domain Name for Your WordPress Site

WORDPRESS PROVIDES A free domain name; however, it'll end with "wordpress.com." You should invest in a domain name. It makes your website look more legitimate, it increases your SEO, and it'll allow you to run ads on it, if you're into that.

A domain name can cost you as little $10 a year or as much as a few thousand dollars! The price largely depends on the perceived value of the domain name. For example, owning the domain AdvertisingNewYork.com would cost substantially more than FultonStreetMarketing.com. In most cases, your domain name will probably cost you between $50 and $100 a year.

Step #2: Choose a Theme from WordPress

YOU'RE FREE TO design and upload your own theme. However, WordPress provides hundreds of free themes and many others that can be purchased for cheap. It might be tempting to use a free theme to save some pennies, but they're generally not as good as the premium ones.

Step #3: Create a Custom Permalink Structure in Common Settings

WHEN YOU SET up a WordPress site, your posts will be perma-linked using a basic, numbered format that doesn't describe what the article is about and doesn't benefit the SEO of your site. To change this, go to "Settings" and "Permalinks" and change the "Common" settings to "Custom Structure." You'll now be able to create your own permalink for each article. For SEO and descriptive purposes, it's best to use the title of the article or content (e.g., yoursite.com/name-of-your-content).

Step #4: Set up All of Your Administrators and Authors

YOU MAY VERY likely have more than one person contribut-ing to your website. In order to add more administrators and authors, go to "Users" and "Add New." Fill out your own infor-mation (i.e., name, username, password, email, etc.). Classify yourself as an administrator. This enables you to create new accounts and have a greater amount of control over your web-site. You should also spend this time setting up the rest of the accounts for your colleagues, assigning them the roles you want for them.

Step #5: Choose Discussion Settings

THE DISCUSSION SETTINGS tab has a few very important options that you know about:

DEFAULT ARTICLE SETTINGS

CHECK THE BOX that notifies others blogs when they've been linked to from an article and the box that allows pingbacks and trackbacks. Both are a great way to increase traffic to your site. Uncheck the final box that allows people to post comments on new articles. This is a useful way to combat spammers.

OTHER COMMENT SETTINGS

CHECK THE FIRST, second, and forth box. This requires users to be logged in and to fill out their information if they want to comment, which is great for building a database.

EMAIL ME WHENEVER

IT'S GOOD TO know when someone has commented on your article. Checking these two boxes notifies you whenever some- one has commented on an article. Furthermore, any comment is held for moderation to make sure that it's appropriate and not spam.

Step #6: Write up Your "About" Page

THE "ABOUT" PAGE should include a description of your company's operations, what you do, your products, your history, and perhaps a brief outline of what's contained on the site. If you have quite a few employees, you should create a second page entitled "Who We Are"—or something similar—that contains a brief biography and accompanying photo of the senior members of your business.

Step #7: Install Plug-Ins

WORDPRESS HAS AN amazing number of plug-ins that can really enhance the overall effectiveness of your site. To download these, copy and paste the name into Google search and download the plug-in from the website. After you've downloaded the plug-ins, drag them into your folder where WordPress is installed, and go to "Plug-ins" and "Add New," then click on the "This Page" link to upload the plug-ins to your WordPress site. You may also use the WordPress search engine for the plug-ins you wish to upload.

Step #8: Create Your Essential Pages

AT THE VERY least, you need the following pages on your site:
- **Home page/landing page:** This page should be well-organized and act as a launching pad for the other pages on your site. It should have strong visuals, a colorful description of yourself, your company, and your mission statement, and a call to action.
- **Products and services page:** This page is supposed to sell your strengths and convince the reader why your business is the best option for their needs. Your product should be

purchased easily, with a guarantee on quality, security, and, if shipping is involved, expediency.

- **About page:** The "About" page tells the viewer your story and what your business, product, and website is about. This may also include your hours of operation and location.
- **Who we are page:** The "Who we are" page lists the senior employees of your company.
- **Contact page:** This page lists the phone number, email address, address, social media sites, and any other information customers would need to contact you.

Step #9: Back up Your WordPress Site

YOU WANT TO make sure all of your files and databases are backed up in case something goes wrong with your site. Purchase or download a back-up plug-in for your WordPress site. BlogVault, VaultPress, CodeGuard, and XCloner are a few of the good back-up plug-ins available. Adding the plug-ins will likely top up your security settings. However, just to be safe, you should go to "Users" and delete the original admin account. Hackers know that this account is automatically assigned generic information, which makes the back end of your site easier to hack. Deleting the original admin account gives your site extra security.

Appendix 2

How to Set up a Facebook Page for Your Business

* * * * * * * *

Step #1: Research Popular Facebook Pages

VIEW FACEBOOK PAGES that you've liked, as well as popular Facebook pages from other businesses. What are they doing right? How often are they posting? What content is best received? Take notes and incorporate their good tactics into your own Facebook page.

Step #2: Set up Your Business Page

YOU PROBABLY HAVE a personal Facebook account, but setting up your Facebook page for your business is very different.

The first thing to keep in mind is your Facebook brand page will be completely controlled from your personal Facebook account.

On the sidebar, under "Pages," click the "More" tab. From there, you can choose to "Create a Page."

You'll be asked, "What type of business are you?" This is your chance to set up the type of business page you want to run. From there, you'll fill in some very basic contact information for your business.

You'll be prompted on the next page to fill out information.

About

THIS IS IMPORTANT. Provide a quick description of your company. What do you do? What makes your company interesting? Make sure you fill in your company web page to direct any visitors back to your site.

You also have the opportunity to choose a unique Facebook URL for people to find your page. Try to think of something simple yet still representative of your brand. If you can't think of anything right away, you'll have a chance to change it again after you create your page. Note that after you leave this page, you can only change it *once*, and then you can never change it again.

Also, make sure you indicate that your business is a *real* establishment, business, or venue. Many people like to create fake brand pages for fun, so this helps companies identify themselves as the real deal. By doing this, you'll have greater access to all of Facebook's page tools later on.

Profile Picture

SELF-EXPLANATORY. FIND A nice photo of your company that's 160 by 160 pixels. We highly recommend using a nice, crisp photo of your brand logo. Unlike the unique Facebook URL, profile pictures can be changed regularly, so no stress here.

Add to Favorites

IF YOU'RE IN charge of many different pages, you can add a page to your Facebook favorites to keep it near the top of your Facebook page. If this is your first page, then you can ignore this for now.

Reach More People

THIS IS AN important step if you're interested in setting up advertising in the future. Take the time to fill out your payment information here so that you're ready to go with Facebook advertising. If not, you can always do this later once you're ready to start advertising.

Step #3: Manage Permissions

WHEN SETTING YOUR permissions, you should allow your page to be as visible and open as possible, because you want to maximize your viewers. You can also specify words or phrases that you want blocked from your page. This is a good way to filter out lewd language and spammers.

Step #4: Fill out Your Basic Information

THIS IS ALL pretty intuitive. It's advisable that you choose your company logo as your main photo. Make sure you add the URL of your website! When filling out the "About" section, pitch your product the same way you would in a pitch. Make it succinct and catchy!

Step #5: Add Important Information

CLICK ON THE "Edit Info" tab to add hours of business, location(s), phone number, email address, and important URLS. You'll also want to write a strong description. Facebook allows enough characters to write an in-depth description.

Step #6: Add Photos

PHOTOS OF YOUR products, building, employees, events, and reviews in newspapers should all be posted on your page.

Step #7: Add Friends and Integrate Your Page with Other Technologies

HERE ARE A few ways to cross-purpose technology and apps.
- Invite friends to your page via Facebook, email, and word of mouth.
- Connect your page to your website and Twitter.
- If you don't have a Facebook app for your phone already, make sure you get one. You never know when you'll need to post something while you're away from the computer.
- Connect your LinkedIn profile to your Facebook page by using the LinkedIn app.
- Tip! Click on the "Get Started" button. It'll offer numerous steps you can take to get the most out of your page.

Step #8: Assign Administrative Roles

FACEBOOK HAS AN "Administrative Roles" option for page administrators. There are five assignable roles: manager, content creator, advertiser, Insights analyst, and moderator. They each have their own distinct permissions clearance, allowing the administrator control over what others can see and change. Furthermore, only the administrator can assign roles.

Step #9: Install the WordPress Plug-in for Your Facebook Page

THE WORDPRESS APP is easy to use, and it allows WordPress bloggers to publish content easily on their Facebook timeline and Facebook pages with no coding. Furthermore, the plug-in enables WordPress users to add additional widgets, such as activity feeds, likes, and subscriptions.

Step #10: Set up Your RSS Blog Feed

IF YOU HAVE a blog, attach the RSS link to your Facebook page. It's a great way to get more followers!

Step #11: Explore the Available Facebook Applications

OF COURSE, HAVING your own Facebook App would be great. However, adding existing apps such as YouTube is an effective way to make your page more attractive.

Step #12: Start Inviting People to Like Your Page

HERE ARE FOUR ways you can get more people to like your page:

- Invite your friends, family, and co-workers to like your page. The more likes your page has, the more influence it has, so use your connections as a foundation for your brand.
- Run some Facebook advertising. Facebook ads are simple to set up and can be designed specifically to increase the number of page likes you have. Test a couple of ads with a small budget before spending too much money.
- Spread the news of your new page on Twitter, Instagram, Tumblr, and any other social media networks you have.
- If you have a newsletter, encourage your readers to like your Facebook page to get the most up-to-date information about your business.

Step #13: Sign up for Facebook for Business

FACEBOOK FOR BUSINESS is a brand new way for businesses to use Facebook. This gives managers a streamlined dashboard to run multiple Facebook pages for different brands or clients at once. This also helps advertisers, as it allows for multiple billing profiles for different ad campaigns. To learn more about Facebook for Business, visit business.facebook.com.

Appendix 3

How to Set up a Twitter Account for Your Business

. . . .

Step #I: Choose a Good Handle

BESIDES YOUR NAME, Twitter also requires that you have a handle name that others can search for. Your handle begins with an at-sign (@); for example, @marketinglocally. Make sure your handle contains full words only. You have only a few characters, so, if your business has a long name, think of a creative way to shorten it without using half words.

Secondly, refrain from using characters or incomplete words in your handle (e.g., @Bob_Smith or @bobsmi instead of the preferable @bobsmith). Both will decrease your SEO because they make it more difficult for new users to find your Twitter page.

You want your Twitter handle to be descriptive and intuitive. Ask yourself, what keywords would others use to find you on Twitter? Most of the time, the answer will be your business name.

Step #2: Write a Good Description

THERE'S ROOM UNDERNEATH your name and handle for a brief description. Use the space to succinctly describe your business and what makes it interesting.

Step #3: Choose a Photo

THE PHOTO THAT accompanies your name and handle should be your logo. You want this image to be recognizable and immediately associated with your business.

Step #4: Choose a Background

WHILE TWITTER PROVIDES background images for your page, you should have your own. Twitter makes this easy: just go to "Settings," "Design," "Customize Your Own," and "Upload Image." Your background should be something that represents your business. Perhaps you have an attractive product that would look great as a background image? Or a team photo of all your employees? You want your page to stand out when people visit it for the first time, so decorate it in a way that shows what's great about your business.

Step #5: Add Links to Your Other Sites

ADD THE URLS of your website, Facebook page, and blog to your Twitter page to increase the number of people who'll follow your other social media sites.

Step #6: Install Twitter Plug-Ins for Your Other Sites

INSTALL TWITTER PLUG-INS or code on your websites and other social media sites. This is a great way to redirect more people to your Twitter page.

Appendix 4

5 Simple Steps for Creating and Maintaining a YouTube Account for Your Business

- - - - - - - - -

Step #1: Create an Account

NOW THAT YOUTUBE and Google+ are parts of the same company, your YouTube account will actually be your Google account! If you don't already have a Google account—or you want to make a professional email or persona for your business—head over to gmail.com to create your new account. Make sure you write down the email and password for this!

Once you create an account, you can now head to YouTube .com and login with your new account information. They'll ask you some basic questions, such as the name you want to use for your channel, but the setup is very simple. Once that's completed, make sure you edit your profile and add all pertinent information about your business. Make sure to populate the "Channel Description" box with information about your business.

Step #2: Customize Your Channel

YOU CAN CHANGE the colors and themes of your page by click-ing on "Settings," "Themes," and "Colors." Uploading JPEGs of your business, staff, or logo is a great way to give your YouTube channel a unique look. If you'd rather use some of the pre-made themes, use colors that reflect your business logo.

Remember that your Google+ account is also an important part of your YouTube channel. If someone were to click on your name for more information inside the channel, they'll be taken directly to your Google+ page. Make sure you fill in your basic information here and update the photos.

Step #3: Delete All Offensive Comments and Respond to All Critical Comments

BY "OFFENSIVE" WE'RE talking about spam, vulgar language, and hurtful comments. Such comments shouldn't be tolerated on your channel, which is what you should post if someone questions your business about the removal of offensive comments. You should not delete critical comments that are complaints about your business or product. Rather, use your channel as a podium to answer any complaints customers may have.

Step #4: Employ Good SEO for Your YouTube Channel

BELIEVE IT OR not, YouTube channels can play a big role in SEO. Here's how you can maximize your visibility.

Title: Your keywords must be in your title. Furthermore, your best and most descriptive keyword needs to be at the front of your title. For example, a proper title for this subsec-tion would be "YouTube SEO Tips for Businesses." A poor title for the same subsection would be "How a Business Can Set Up Great SEO for Their YouTube."

Description: The same rules apply for your description as for your title. Insert as many keywords as possible. Try to use key phrases that people might use when searching for videos pertaining to your content.

Keyword tags: Use the same keywords you used in your title and description. Maintaining consistency in your keywords is better for your SEO. Furthermore, using too many keywords might damage your SEO, as search engines punish sites that stuff their site with too many keywords.

Internal linking: Similar to a website, internally linking from another site to your YouTube page increases your SEO ranking. Inserting links into your videos that redirect users to related content boosts a video's search result ranking.

Comments: Request feedback from viewers. The more people comment on a video, the greater its SEO. Users will likely use the same keywords in their comments that are used for the video. Further, commentary is shown on the commenter's own page, which increases the amount of links redirected to your site.

Auto-captions: YouTube is able to insert captions automatically based on a speech recognition software. Captions allow viewers who are hard of hearing to watch your videos. What's more, YouTube takes into account captions as part of keyword SEO! To enable captions, go to "Settings," "Playback," "Setup," "Captions," and "Always Show Automatic Captions." Auto-caption will occasionally transcribe text incorrectly. Before posting your video, review the captions and make sure there are no issues. If there are, simply go to the "Editing" page. Any changes you make to the captions will override the auto-captions feature.

Step #5: Promote Your Videos on Your Other Social Media

PROMOTING YOUR WEBSITE through your other social sites is a great way to promote your videos and redirect people to your YouTube channel. Install a YouTube plug-in for your WordPress site, tweet, and post on your Facebook wall whenever you have a video you want consumers to watch.

Embedding videos into your website might have been a challenge some years ago. Nowadays, video sharing platforms, such as YouTube or Vimeo, make it fairly easy to show a video on your website. This service costs nothing and it gives you the advantage of hosting your video on their server, using their bandwidth.

On YouTube, for example, underneath the video, you'll find the "Share" button. By clicking on that button, several options will appear. Here you can find the HTML code used to embed a link that you can then share or post on your website.

Video is displayed below. However, to embed the video directly into a website, you have to click on the button "Embed."

Once you've done this, a box with the embed code will appear. Now just copy this code by using the right mouse click and select "Copy." Open the source code of your website and paste it into your page (again by using the right mouse click and selecting "paste"). The embed code will be deposited into your website. Save and publish the changes and view it on your website!

It works with almost all browsers, and, if not, the visitor will be prompted by the browser to download the appropriate software.

YouTube even provides a service to customize how the video window should look and behave. You're able to select a checkbox for each option directly below the spot where the embedded code appears.

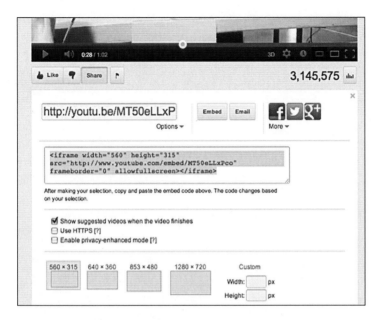

You might include related videos when the video finishes. You might use HTTPS—a more secure protocol—or enable YouTube's privacy enhanced mode, which allows people to watch the video without keeping information in cookies related to the videos they've viewed.

You can also select the size of the window in which the video is shown. YouTube allows you to choose between four sizes.

Appendix 5

Building Your Marketing Plan

• • • • • • • •

BEFORE BIG BANKS will finance your business, you need to show them you know what you're doing. You need to demonstrate your implementation plan, your five-year plan, your contingencies, and so on. Even if you don't anticipate going to the bank, having a marketing plan is never a bad idea. Here's a breakdown of all the elements in of our marketing plans. Feel free to adapt this for your own company.

Title Page

MAKE SURE TO list the person or people in charge and the name of the product, project, or initiative right at the top. If you're reviewing old projects, you want to be sure you have a relevant point of contact.

Executive Summary

WHAT'S YOUR MARKETING plan in a page or less? Shareholders or executives won't have time to go through your report page by page, so make sure you can summarize everything you want to do in a single page.

Research and Analysis

THE SIZE OF this section will be completely dependent on the type of plan you're doing. As a rule of thumb, every business decision you make should have some sort of research or fact-finding to back it up. If you're planning on expanding into a new market, where's the evidence that proves the new market will be receptive to your business?

If you've conducted any first-person research, like focus groups and surveys, be sure to include the findings here. What do the results mean? Make sure your recommendations flow organically from your research results.

Targeting

CLEARLY STATE WHO your target market is and why they're your target market. Go beyond just talking about demographics and geographics, and talk about their behavior. Are you targeting eighteen-year-old males who sit at home, study all day, and buy things from the Internet, or the eighteen-year-old male who spends all his time partying with his friends? Two identical demographics can hide two very different lifestyles.

What are your main competitors for this target market? Every group of consumers has their own personal preferences, so try to figure out who your biggest rivals are for your product category.

Recommendations

THIS SHOULD BE the bulk of your marketing plan. Based on your research, what are you planning on doing? More importantly, how are you planning on doing it? It might seem traditional, but refer to the four P's here. Most marketing plans generally have two to three recommendations.

- **Product (or service):** What are you selling? Why does your target market want it?
- **Price:** How much does your product or service cost? Are you priced as a luxury brand or a value brand? Remember to compare prices with your direct competitors as well.
- **Placement:** Where can you be found? For products, being part of a strong distribution network can make or break your company. If you haven't secured any deals or partnerships yet, list out who you'd want to partner with, and why.
- **Promotion:** How will people know about your product? Go into all the different avenues of advertising you think might work, as well as their price points.
- **Measurement:** This isn't one of the four P's, but it's crucial to list out exactly how you measure success for this recommendation. Will it be the number of sales per year? Market share? Conversions? These goals will be time-sensitive, so hold yourself accountable to them once the project takes off.

Risk Analysis

NO ONE CAN predict exactly what will go wrong with your project, but it pays to figure out what your contingency plan is beforehand. I like to list all the things that could go wrong with any particular idea (e.g., it rains on an event day, no one shows up, partnerships fall through, etc.) and detail how likely and severe they would be. Make sure you talk about what you plan to do *if* something goes wrong and which member of your team is assigned to take responsibility in that case.

Conclusion

WHICH OF YOUR recommendations is the best? Using your expertise, suggest one recommendation you think will have the highest chance of succeeding and explain why. If you're writing this for your superiors, stakeholders, or partners, they may have their own ideas—which is why I encourage you to list a few recommendations—but it's always a good idea to highlight your first choice.

Glossary

· · · · · · · · ·

A/B testing: Comparing two different variations of an advertisement or landing page to see which one is more effective.

advertising: A notice or announcement in a public medium promoting a product, service, or event or publicizing a job vacancy. Usually paid for, although free advertising isn't unheard of.

affiliate marketing: A type of online marketing where an advertiser rewards other sites for hosting their ads. Whenever someone clicks an advertisement, the site that hosted the ad is paid a commission.

AdWords: Google's ad delivery network. It's split into search ads (i.e., text ads that appear in Google searches) and display ads (i.e., banner ads that show up all over the Internet).

analytics: A detailed breakdown of your website, marketing campaign, or advertising results. Most commonly this would be done through Google Analytics.

banner ad: An online graphic advertisement that encourages people to click it. These are typically used in conjunction with PPC campaigns.

board: A collection of pinned photos on your Pinterest account. You can collect different images by pinning them to specific boards for yourself or your followers.

call to action: A clear message in your advertising that encourages the viewer to take some sort of action. This could be to sign up on a contact form, call your number, or buy your products.

content: Information written for the purpose of being read, watched, or enjoyed. From a business standpoint, content is useful for attracting new customers.

conversion: Someone who completed your goal in an advertising campaign, whether that's a completed sale, liking your Facebook page, signing up for your mailing list, etc.

click-through: A click-through—or click—is when someone clicks on your ad or post online.

cost-per-click (CPC): The total amount of money spent for every person who clicks on your ad.

cost-per-impression (CPI): The total amount of money spent for every impression on your ad.

direct mail: Mailing out advertisements to prospects directly through the postal system (AKA snail mail). Tends to be more expensive than other marketing initiatives, but can be effective for some target markets.

engagement: Someone interacting with your brand. For social media, this includes likes, comments, and shares.

impressions: The number of times your ad is seen.

inbound marketing: A type of marketing designed to increase website traffic and new leads.

Insights: Facebook's analytics tool available to business page managers.

hashtag: The pound key (#) used in several social media platforms to show what your message is about. For example, adding #Dogs would be seen by anyone searching for dogs.

HTML: A computer language that allows users to create and design websites.

keywords: The theme of any individual page of the Internet. Google and other search engines look at your page and determine what the keywords are and use that to figure out how relevant your page is.

landing pages: A simple one-page webpage that is used to generate leads. People are usually encouraged to sign up for a mailing list, purchase a product, or speak with a representative. A popular tactic by marketers is to offer a free gift (such as a white paper, an informative video, or a guide) in return for user participation.

lead: A potential customer who has taken interest in your business or your products.

media buying: The purchase of an advertisement from an established media network, such as radio and TV.

mention: On Twitter, a mention is when someone includes your Twitter handle (e.g., @Curvecomms) in a tweet. You'll receive a notification if someone mentions you in this way.

mobile optimization: Designing your website so that it looks good on mobile phones. See *responsive design*.

pay-per-click (PPC): Unlike CPC, which is a general metric of ad performance, PPC usually refers to using a large advertiser like Google or Facebook, where they are paid every time someone clicks on your ad.

placement: One of the 4 P's of marketing. Refers to the distribution channels where your product will be sold.

price: One of the 4 P's of marketing. The amount you will charge for your product or service. Higher prices will reduce the total number of sales, but may make your product appear luxurious.

product: One of the 4 P's of marketing. What you will actually be selling. It is important to consider what benefits your product provides to customers.

promotion: One of the 4 P's of marketing. Promotion covers all the marketing initiatives associated with your product. This encompasses advertising, PR, media buying, social media, etc.

public relations (PR): The practice of managing the spread of information between an individual or an organization and the public.

reach: The number of unique people who have seen your ad.

reblog: A feature of Tumblr that allows you to send someone else's content to your fans. See *retweet.*

return on investment (ROI): What your reward is for investing in something. A high ROI means your investment was a success.

responsive design: Building your website so that it works well on all devices and resolutions.

retweet: On Twitter, a copy of your tweet that someone else sends on their account. This helps to boost the reach of the original tweet and establish your relevancy to your followers.

search engine optimization (SEO): The practice of making your websites more attractive to search engines. This includes, but is not limited to, making sure each and every page has a different keyword, adding a meta description, adding proper headers, and ensuring your site has plenty of high-quality backlinks.

social media: A website or application that allows users to create and share content or network. For businesses, social media is a platform that allows for easy, two-way conversations between two different people.

target market: The group of people who are expected to buy your product. A well-defined target market should be defined by demographics, geographics, and behavior.

viral: When a piece of content you create becomes incredibly popular on the web through organic sharing.

Acknowledgments

· · · · · · · ·

THIS BOOK WOULD not have been possible without support from the Curve Communications team. Special credit to Justin Wong, who worked closely with me on much of the content in this book, and to Gina Robinson, Heather Roy, Kerry Slater, Alastair Hubbard, Connor Barnsley, and Cora Schupp, who all helped with their own expertise in marketing.

Also thanks to the Page Two Strategies principals, Trena White and Jesse Finkelstein, and their entire team, especially Scott Steedman.

GEORGE AFFLECK is the president and CEO of Curve Communications, a fifteen-year-old marketing firm that has worked with hundreds of small businesses, non-profits, and event organizers. Curve Communications prides itself on innovation and was one of the first North American advertising agencies to adopt a social media approach to PR and communications. Before launching Curve, Affleck was a host and reporter on public radio. He has been a city councillor since 2011.